CONFEDERATE CHAPLAIN
A War Journal

Father James B. Sheeran in later life as pastor in Morristown, N. J.

Confederate Chaplain

A WAR JOURNAL

of

Rev. James B. Sheeran, c.ss.r.
14th Louisiana, C.S.A.

Edited by
REV. JOSEPH T. DURKIN, S.J.

With a Preface by
BRUCE CATTON

THE BRUCE PUBLISHING COMPANY
MILWAUKEE

Library of Congress Catalog Card Number: 60–15430
© 1960 THE BRUCE PUBLISHING COMPANY
MADE IN THE UNITED STATES OF AMERICA

PREFACE

Although the Army of Northern Virginia has long since passed beyond the horizon, it somehow retains its reality. Its character and its personality survive. From the testimony of many obscure men who lived with this army, sharing its hardships, its dreams, its victories, and its final defeat, we get materials for a sober history which is just as moving as the romantic myths say it was. This army's legend is built around a hard core of truth.

Among the pieces of testimony that were left for our generation, not the least important is this journal written by the Reverend Father James Sheeran, Catholic chaplain, good campaigner, and one of the most dedicated of Southern patriots. His day-by-day account of what he saw and did during three years with the Army of Northern Virginia will appeal both to the general reader and to the serious student of the Civil War. It helps to round out the picture of the army, of some of its distinguished officers, and of certain of its opponents. Quite incidentally, it gives an appealing picture of its author, who appears to have been an outspoken person well worth knowing.

Father Sheeran detested the Yankee invader as hotly as any Confederate could. He refers to the Federal troops, on one occasion, as "Lincoln's bandits," and his references to General Phil Sheridan, who put him in a noisome military prison, are as caustic as anything you will readily find. He had a quaint habit of exhorting any Yankee prisoners he met; it appears that he tried to convert them, not to his own religious faith but to a realization of the justice and rightness of the Confederate cause. In the Gettysburg campaign he proudly noted that although his fellow Confederates did make away with a lot of Pennsylvania chickens and a good deal of garden truck they indulged in none

v

of the wanton destruction which Federal soldiers had inflicted on Virginia. Of the Pennsylvania farmers on whom his comrades levied toll, Father Sheeran wrote loftily that they were a loutish folk: "With all their wealth they appear little advanced in civilization."

His primary concern, of course, was for the immortal souls of the soldiers whom he was serving, and his priestly duties kept him very busy — celebrating Mass, delivering sermons, hearing confessions, ministering to the sick and the wounded, and waging unending war on such camp vices as profanity, drunkenness, and gambling. He had, too, it would seem, all of the instincts of a soldier; on occasion he could round up a flock of stragglers, form a firing line, and keep it in action until some combat officer could be found to take charge of it.

Some of his pictures of the army in action are memorable. He went with A. P. Hill's division on the famous forced march from Harper's Ferry to the battlefield of Antietam, and he reported that at least half of the men in this division, if not more than half, fell out along the way and never got to the field until the battle was over. Most of these were men who had simply been driven beyond human endurance, but too many, he felt, were malingerers — and this in the crack combat division of Lee's army. Father Sheeran gloomily believed that Lee might actually have won at Antietam if his men had not straggled so badly. Proud as he was of this army, he never pretended that it was made up exclusively of stainless sons of light.

A month after Antietam, noting how rest and a thorough refit had improved army morale and restored its numbers, the chaplain felt that the army was in better shape than it had been in for three months — an interesting footnote on the overcaution of the Union commander, General George B. McClellan, whose failure to press Lee vigorously made this rejuvenation possible.

His vignette of Hill's men during the retreat from Gettysburg deserves a place in any history of Lee's army. Despite what they had been through, these soldiers went back to Virginia in high spirits, laughing at incidents of the retreat, clowning it up occasionally to relieve the tedium of the long hike: "To hear them you would think they were going to a party of pleasure instead of retreating from a hard-fought battle."

Father Sheeran's journal shares one thing with most of the enduring personal-experience accounts of the Civil War; under everything, the real enemy appears to be war itself, and not just the opposing army. His anger really makes him eloquent when he denounces the mulish stupidity of incompetent troop commanders, the greed of supply officers who live comfortably while the soldiers go hungry and unclad, the impersonal brutality of the military machine, and the profiteering of civilians who make a good thing out of the war while the fighting men bleed and die. Traveling across the South in the middle of the war, Father Sheeran wrote angrily: "I found the stay-at-homes having but one great object in view, that is, the making of money. Never had I seen such avariciousness." How many Federal diarists wrote in exactly the same terms about the stay-at-homes on their own side!

In the final despairing months of the winter of 1864-1865, the chaplain spent some time in Richmond, and he was particularly enraged by the gentlemen of the Confederate Congress, who, he felt, should be held up to "the contempt and scorn of all future generations." By that time the cause was dying and there probably was not a great deal the Congress could have done about it, but Father Sheeran's verdict is unsparing: "They helped much to murder a nation which was winning for itself one of the proudest and most honorable names on record. . . . They were great men only in one sense: great in their ignorance and powers to do mischief."

It has been said that the Confederate soldier was one of the most rugged individualists in American history. As rugged as any of them, surely, was this chaplain. It is good to get acquainted with him.

— BRUCE CATTON

FATHER SHEERAN AND HIS JOURNAL

Born in Ireland at Temple Mehill, County Longford, in 1819, James Sheeran at the age of twelve emigrated to Canada, spent two years there, and then came to New York City and later to McConnellsville, Pennsylvania. Moving westward, he was, by 1845, in the tailoring business in Monroe, Michigan. There is some indication that he had previously studied law, but, apparently, he never practiced that profession. At Monroe he also taught in the boys' school operated by the Redemptorist Fathers. About 1842 (the exact date is not known) he married and had a son* and a daughter. (His wife's name has not been ascertained.) Having become a widower in 1849, he sent his little girl to board with the Sisters of the Immaculate Heart and devoted himself more and more to his teaching work. In 1855 he joined the Redemptorist Congregation, and after three years' study of philosophy and theology was ordained to the priesthood on September 18, 1858. Less than four months before this event his daughter, having entered the convent, had received the habit of the Immaculate Heart Sisters.** 1861 found Father Sheeran stationed at the Redemptorist Church in New Orleans. He had been there for almost three years and had become an ardent Southerner in his thoughts and affections. When his Father Provincial asked for volunteers to act as chaplains for the Confederate Army, he leaped at the opportunity and on September 2, 1861, was assigned to the Army of Northern Virginia.

During his period of wartime service Father Sheeran kept a journal, the larger and most significant portion of which is here presented. The record is important not mainly as a commentary on the military events proper. Campaigns and battles are, of course, what the journal is about.

---

* The subsequent history of the son is veiled in obscurity.

** A slight chronological difficulty is involved in Father Sheeran's account of the life of his daughter. He tells us that she died in the convent in February, 1861, a few months before her eighteenth birthday. This would make her in September, 1858, about fifteen years old, too young to take her vows as a nun. She would be old enough, however, to begin her noviceship.

But, with a few exceptions, it contains no new or particularly pene-
trating analyses of military tactics or strategy.

Rather, the worth of the journal lies in two qualities it possesses to a
high degree. First, it is a revelation of a unique and admirable character
— that of a priest, totally devoted to his duty, absolutely fearless, and
ardently, according to his lights, patriotic. He had, it must be admitted,
some traits that seem quite angular; but his sincerity and spirit of dedica-
tion were equal to those of Robert E. Lee.

Second, the journal gives us some genre pictures of military life that
are vivid, fascinating, and often humorous. So true is this that the reader
may well conclude that the net effect of the journal is to portray the
atmosphere of the war more forcibly than if the stress had been placed
on tactics and strategy.

Whatever the virtues and defects of the journal, it is certainly a Civil
War document of considerable importance. A poet has spoken of "magic
casements opening on faery scenes forlorn." Father Sheeran's record is
indeed an additional casement affording a fresh outlook on the Civil
War. He shows us no faery spectacles, although the picture is sometimes
forlorn; but it is always interesting.

Note on the Character of the Journal and the Method of the Editor

Father Sheeran's journal consists of two handwritten volumes bound
in imitation khaki-colored velvet and recording his campaigns and other
war experiences and observations on the war from August, 1862, to his
return to his parish in New Orleans in 1865.

His method of composing the journal was as follows:

Usually while in the field on active duty and during his furlough trip
to the deep South and his period of imprisonment, he kept day-by-day
records, probably on rough slips of paper. These at the first opportunity
he would rewrite and often expand in the journal described above. He
writes, for example, under date of "Jan.–Mar. 1863": "Whilst convalescent
[at Richmond] I have written out notes taken during the summer
campaign."

At other times he would take no notes on the actual days the events
occurred, but would do so very shortly afterward. He tells us, for in-
stance, "Being now on the Virginia side of the river, I halted and wrote
my notes on the battle of Sharpsburg" (*Journal,* p. 182).

A few times in the latter part of the journal he combines the former of these two methods with another procedure: he does the rewriting in the form of a letter sent to his ward in Richmond and also copied verbatim in the journal.

The employment of these literary devices results often in inaccuracies or inconsistencies in the dating of the entries. It is difficult, at times, to ascertain whether in the diary a date refers to the day on which an incident occurred, or whether it is the day on which the Chaplain is retrospectively narrating the incident. In other instances, the date he puts down is clearly that of the incident and the day on which he recorded the incident; in other words, he is recopying his original note in its original form.

Hence, for purposes of clarity, the present editor has omitted all of Father Sheeran's indications of dates and has inserted the actual date of occurrence of each incident mentioned. Remembering the chaplain's methods as above outlined, this seems to be sufficient, while at the same time averting confusion on the part of the reader.

Father Sheeran's peculiarities of spelling have been retained.

CONTENTS

CONFEDERATE CHAPLAIN
A War Journal

THE JOURNAL

1862

In the midsummer of 1862 Father Sheeran was at Gordonsville, Virginia, with the 14th Louisiana Regiment, Ewell's* Division, Jackson's Corps.

This was the military situation at the beginning of that August in the eastern theater of war: McClellan's drive against Richmond had been balked, temporarily at least, by Lee's stubborn army on the Peninsula, the naval defenses on the James, and Jackson's hit-and-run tactics in the Valley. Shifting their strategy, the Federals were now launching an invasion of Virginia from the north; Pope,** with a force of 47,000 men, was already ninety miles above Richmond. McClellan was coming up to meet him for a combined attack on the Confederate capital.

Lee had daringly decided to defend Richmond by weakening his own position there and throwing Jackson forward to hit Pope before the latter was joined by McClellan. On August 2 Jackson, with only 24,000 men, was at Gordonsville, thirty miles south of Pope's advanced position at Culpeper.

Father Sheeran's diary begins at this point. He reported at Gordonsville to General Ewell who received him warmly:

Aug. 2   The General expressed much pleasure at having a Catholic chaplain in his Division and suggested that my orderly should be mounted to aid me more efficiently in time of an engagement. I told him the difficulty I would have to procure a horse; but this difficulty was soon removed by a suggestion that I should tell the boys

* Lieutenant General Richard Stoddert Ewell, C.S.A.
** Brevet Major General John Pope, U.S.A.

1

to capture me one at the next battle. . . . (As a consequence my orderly was mounted after the subsequent battle of Manassa [sic].)

During the next few days Father Sheeran was able to hear many confessions, celebrated Mass each morning, and distributed many Holy Communions. By August 7 Pope had begun his advance against Jackson, who calmly moved up to block him. Father Sheeran's description is more personalized:

Aug. 7   Having found out the position of the Yankees, Ewell's whole Division crosses Liberty Bridge about 4 P.M. in pursuit of Pope and his Abolition Robbers.

Father Sheeran keeps his eyes open as the army makes its march:

Aug. 8   The devastating marks of the enemy were visible along

Approach-   our route. The fences were torn down, corn trampled

ing the   under foot, and houses gutted of their furniture.

Rapidan

from

south

As will be seen frequently in this journal, Father Sheeran's Southern partisanship was vehement and inclined to believe the worst of the enemy, to whom he usually referred in terms less than complimentary. He lent a willing ear to an indignant Virginia citizen:

Aug. 8   The owner of [a farm], a gentleman of high standing,

Just north gave us some heartrending accounts of the savage and

of the   barbarous treatment he and his family had received

Rapidan   from Lincoln's bandits. They plundered him of all he had; his corn, wheat, and pork, killed his hogs, drove off his beef cattle and even his milch cows. They threw down his fences, and would not allow his negro servants to put them up unless he would pay them regular wages, thus exposing the growing crops to destruction. They even threatened to shoot this gentleman for having a loaded musket in his house. . . . The day was oppressively warm and the march for some three hours being very rapid, many of our men were broken down and some even sunstruck. . . . We met General Jackson riding alone. . . . It was the first time I ever saw him, and such was his plain attire that, had I not been informed, I never would have taken him for a commissioned officer.

On August 9 the two armies clashed at Cedar Run and Cedar Mountain. The battle followed one of the classic patterns of Jackson's tactics. With his left and center broken by the initial onslaught, the imperturbable Stonewall re-formed his line, counterattacked on both flanks, and drove back the Federals who were under the command of General N. P. Banks. Father Sheeran reports the decisive last moments of the battle:

Aug. 9   The Irish Battalion of Jackson's old Brig. and a few regiments were in the advance on the Left, the remainder of our forces were concealed in the woods some two hundred yards to the rear. The Yankees pressed upon our advance with overpowering numbers. The Irish Brig., soon abandoned by their companions who were unable to withstand the terrible fire of the advancing enemy, for some time boldly withstood the unequal contest, and only returned [retired?] when their ranks were weakened by the loss of many of their bravest members.

The enemy now confident of victory over our Left wing advanced rapidly after what they supposed our retreating columns, until they were within fifty yards of the woods where the greatest part of Jackson's old Div. were concealed. It was now our turn to charge. As they advanced yelling furiously, they were hailed by a tremendous volley of musketry that mowed them down by regiments. Our boys with a victorious hurrah! which echoed along our lines, start after the retreating enemy shooting them down in great numbers and taking some seven hundred prisoners. Thus ended at about sunset the celebrated infantry contest at the celebrated Battle of Cedar Mountain.

★   ★   ★

Aug. 10 [On the next night] having the wounded of our Div. Hospital properly cared for, Dr. White* and I resolved to go over the battle-field to see if there were any of our men not brought off. Mounting our horses about eleven P.M. we directed our way to the scene of the carnage. . . . I spoke to the wounded and told them to have patience until daylight and we would have them removed and cared for. I met with one poor fellow who was some distance from any of his companions and asked him what regiment he belonged to? "The 73rd N. Y." was the reply. "What's your name?" "P. Sullivan." "Are you a Catholic?" "Yes, I am." "Pat, what brought you here?" "O! Misfortune," was the poor fellow's answer. He had his leg broken by a musket ball.

We passed some two hours travelling over the field, now drenched with the blood of the victims of fanaticism, tyranny and injustice. . . .

Aug. 11 I spent the afternoon among the wounded prisoners we had carried from the field. Among them were two captains of more than ordinary attainments. One of them was very desirous of discussing the war and its

* Probably Archer C. White, listed in the Confederate Register as hospital steward for the 29th Virginia Infantry. There was also an A. J. White, listed as hospital steward in the Army of Northern Virginia.

probable consequences. I, of course, had no objection. I devoted to the Capt. about an hour of my time during which I introduced him into a world of ideas altogether different from that in which he had hitherto been travelling. He denied that he was in favor of Lincoln's administration, maintaining that he was fighting only for the preservation of the Constitution. My parting advice to him was this: "My very good man before going to bed every night try and recall to your memory the number of times Abe Lincoln has perjured himself by violating the Constitution since his introduction into office; then put your hand to your breast and ask yourself in the presence of God, if in fighting for your perjured President, you are fighting for the Constitution of your country." I now bade my Yankee friend goodbye but soon received a messenger from him asking me to favor him with my card. I of course replied with this request.

Jackson now withdrew his forces to Gordonsville, and for days puzzled the Federals by apparently disappearing. But the most brilliant Confederate stroke was yet to come. While Lee, now up at Gordonsville, kept Pope engaged in front, the fast-moving Jackson swept clear around the right wing of the Union Army and planted himself at Manassas Junction. The daring tactic — a near-miracle of deception — cut Pope off from McClellan's advance and jockeyed him into a corner — carefully chosen by Jackson — where he was forced to stand and fight.

Father Sheeran accompanied the troops on this famous march. On the day before they started, he said Mass for his boys:

Aug. 15   . . . a large congregation and many communicants. From the large number attending Mass I cherished the
At Camp Wheat, a few miles south of Cedar Mountain hope that if we should get a few days rest I would have an opportunity of preparing all the Catholic soldiers of our Brig. to meet their God as well as to meet their foe. The interest I feel in the cause for which our brave men are sacrificing the comforts of society and

periling their lives as well as the salvation of their souls prompted me to do all in my power to keep them in the friendship of their God, for I had learned by personal observation that no men fight more bravely than Catholics who approach the sacraments before battle, while on the contrary, there are none more cowardly (save those intensely worthless) than the Catholic whose conscience reproves him of *mortal sin*.

★   ★   ★

Aug. 16   But I was not permitted to realize my fond hope, for on Saturday Aug. 16 at 2 in the morning orders were given to cook two days rations, and to be ready to march at daylight. The whole camp was soon in motion. At daylight, rations being cooked, tents struck and wagons loaded our boys were in rank. As we had to bring up the rear of the Corps in this day's march we had to wait for the other division to pass which took to 10 A.M. This thing of standing so long under arms is one of the most trying to our men, and it is not to be wondered at, that they offered *some* of *their* prayers for those whom they supposed to be the cause of the delay. However, about ten o'clock we moved off and after a rapid march of 15 miles under a burning hot sun encamped for the night some two miles from Orange C. H.

Here again we had the luxury of a gravelly bed, the fence and rails for pillows. We had also an excellent opportunity for making astronomical observations, as the moon and the stars were shedding their brilliant lustre copiously upon us, and consequently were visible from our spacious chamber with [without?] the aid of instruments. But the time and circumstances were not so favorable for prayer, as the men of our brigade were crowded closely together, and they are noted for their loquacity. However, the gravelly *feathers* on which we were endeavoring to repose our wearied bodies, disposed us better for meditation. I thought frequently of those heroes of mortification, whose names adorn the calendar of the Church. St. Rose of Lima choosing a log of wood for a pillow and the bare ground for a couch, and also the other saints who practised similar mortifications, recurred to my memory. I fear however these meditations did not profit me much; for instead of giving the Saints credit for their austerities I considered these very mortifications as child's play compared with what Confederate soldiers had to endure and I of course, among the latter. Happy would we have been or at least thought ourselves that night had we a round log for a pillow, or smooth ground for a bed. But, Oh! Just think of it! A sharp fence rail under your head and rocks from the size of an egg to that of a cannon ball under the wearied body.

Sunday,   . . . I heard of two Virginia soldiers who were to
Aug. 17   be shot for desertion. I hastened to the place of execution and found them surrounded by two Protestant chaplains. Unwilling to witness their execution I returned to camp.

Jackson's great flanking movement was executed to perfection. Marching almost due north and keeping the mountains as a screen on his right, and using Longstreet as a decoy, he reached Salem on August 26. Making a sharp turn southeast, he slipped across the Blue Ridge at Thoroughfare Gap and later that same day was at Bristoe Station, two miles from Manassas Junction.

It is evident that his strategic aims were hidden as successfully from his own army as from the enemy. On the way up his soldiers were grumbling, as Father Sheeran phrases it, that he "could have got between Pope's army and the Rappahannock, and captured that very bad man and his legion of robbers" (Aug. 18). As for the chaplain himself, "I gave myself no concern about it, for I knew that Lee, Jackson and Longstreet knew what they were about."

On one occasion, indeed, Father Sheeran even contributed (as he at first thought) a service beyond the ordinary call of duty:

Aug. 22   Being very tired I sought a place beyond the range of the enemy's guns and then threw myself on the ground to await the arrival of the Dr. As the guns of the enemy were soon silenced the stragglers behind, thinking themselves secure, sat down to rest in the shade of the woods. Here we were enjoying the luxury of the cool shade, when suddenly a great commotion was heard in the direction [from] which we had come. The cry was raised, "The Yankees are coming! ! !" But I paid no attention to it, thinking it was a false alarm made by the colored servants down in the woods, and expressed myself accordingly. This allayed the excitement for the moment. But soon again was heard the cry "The Yankees!" Soon our ambulance drivers, who had just come up as well as our stragglers, were for stampeding. Mounting my *Grey* and riding down to the ambulances I ordered the drivers to move forward as quickly as possible. They obeyed promptly. As I saw no commissioned officer present I took command of the stragglers, and formed them in a line on a road running through the woods. The commanding officer gave orders to reserve fire till the enemy was within short range and then [to] let them have it. The Yankees were advancing very cautiously through the woods. I rode up to our battery to inform the brave Capt. D Kin [?] of the La. G. B. of their approach.* When riding along I cast my eye to the left, and lo! who did I behold? Gen.

---

* An ambiguous passage. The name of the captain may be Dakin. The journal's chirography at this point gives no help. The same is true of the mysterious reference to "the La. G. B.," which *may* mean, "the La. Guards Battery." There was a 1st Sergeant T. J. Dakin in the 2nd Battalion (State Troops), Mississippi Infantry.

Trimble* with his whole brigade drawn up in line
of battle, anticipating the very movement of the enemy
which I and my brave stragglers were preparing to repel.

This was the first time I ever acted as commander,
and I must confess that I felt not a little crestfallen
when I discovered that I was observed by no less a
person than Gen. Trimble. I am certain that the Gen.
with all his gravity must have laughed heartily at my
maneuvering. I informally resigned my office and
retired at a little distance to await the result.

Arrived at Bristoe, Jackson learned that Yankee reinforcements for
Pope were expected to arrive there soon by train. At once the Louisiana
Brigade was placed in line of battle along the railroad:

Aug. 26   The main column of the corps was commanded to halt.
This command was obeyed by the advanced Brigades
without reluctance, but not so with those bringing up
the rear; for all were anxious to see "the fun."

All were now waiting with the most intense anxiety;
when suddenly the whistle of a locomotive in the direction of Warrenton, was heard in the distance; after
a few moments' silence, the whistle was more distinctly
heard to our right in the woods; and scarcely had the
sound died away, when the engine with a long train of
passengers came puffing slowly up to the station. The
engineer perceiving his danger but too late put on all
steam, and ran with rapidity past our line, but not
without receiving a volley from our boys, which sent
him to some place in the other world; but the engine
having up a full head of steam made the escape pretty
well, bored however by the shower of musket balls. This
was but the first of five trains which had brought up
reinforcements to Pope at Warrenton and were now on

* Major General I. R. Trimble, C.S.A.

their return for more. [Bristoe is on the railroad between Manassa and Warrenton, about four miles from
the former.] Jackson was determined that no more of
these precious locomotives should escape. He and a few
men from the ranks placed obstructions on the road
near the bridge. He now walked slowly along the lines
and in a low voice told the boys not to waste their ammunition for he had everything fixed. Soon the whistle
of another engine was heard in the same direction and
as no signal was given to stop at this way station she
dashed along with the usual speed until in front of our
La. boys who, forgetful or rather unmindful of the
order, poured a volley of musketry into her boiler
causing the steam to go in every direction. No sooner
had she received this salutation than she moved with
full force against the obstructions, which cast her off the
road into a ravine and buried Abe Lincoln deep in the
mud. [Abe was the name of the locomotive.] The loud
shouts of our boys made the welkins ring.

From the noise of the musketry I feared some of our
men might be wounded, so I was anxious to get to the
front, for I was now a mile from the station with our
surgeons and ambulances. It was now dark and the
road in some places was very steep, rough and pretty
well blocked up with troops and ordnance wagons. For
a person with the best of sight it would be no easy matter to make his way to the station; but for me it was
rather a dangerous undertaking. However trusting to
the better sight of my horse, and his well known judg-
ment in seeking roads in our frequent night travels, I
in company with the Dr. started for Bristow. We advanced but a short distance, when the noise of another
locomotive was heard; soon the report of another volley

and a tremendous Hurra! were heard to respond — another locomotive had shared the fate of its predecessor.

★   ★   ★

While the Louisianians were disrupting train service at Bristoe Station, another brigade had advanced to Manassas Junction and, after a brief but sharp engagement, captured the valuable Union stores there. The Louisiana brigade, now heavily attacked at Bristoe, fell back to Manassas, where Jackson now concentrated his little army. While this movement was being made, Father Sheeran visited General Ewell (Aug. 27.) — "I conversed freely with him, and heard him bestow some high encomiums on my men." The journal then continues:

Aug. 27   I was not long... in discovering the object of Jackson's visit to Manassa. The storehouses were crowded with provisions of all kinds; on the R.R. was a train nearly a mile in length, laden with commissary stores and supplies of all kinds for Pope's army. I will not attempt to describe the scene I here witnessed for I am sure it beggars description. Just imagine about 6000 men hungry and almost naked, let loose on some million dollars worth of biscuit, cheese, ham, bacon, messpork, coffee, sugar, tea, fruit, brandy, wine, whiskey, oysters; coats, pants, shirts, caps, boots, shoes, socks, blankets, tents etc. etc. Here you would see a crowd enter a car with their old Confed. greys and in a few moments come out dressed in Yankee uniforms; some as cavalry; some as infantry; some as artillerists; others dressed in the splendid uniform of Federal officers. In another place you would see the cavalry helping themselves to new saddles, bridles, spurs, and other necessary equipment. Again you would see our wagoners and ambulance drivers with new sets of harness of every description and curry combs, brushes, sponges, waterpails etc. etc. In another place you would see them distributing canteens.

Here you would see the surgeons loading their wagons with medicine of every description as well as surgical instruments, wines, and brandies of the best quality. Here again were our wagoners loading their teams with crackers, bacon, salt, sugar, coffee etc. etc. Again you would see colored servants carrying off bags of oats for their horses and then returning for personal plunder.

I had often read of the sacking of cities by a victorious army but never did I hear of a railroad train being sacked. I viewed this scene for almost two hours with the most intense anxiety. I saw the whole army become what appeared to me an ungovernable mob, drunk, some few with liquor but the others with excitement. I rode frequently through the surging crowd, viewing them sometimes with a smile, again with a look of sadness. As night approached, the thought of the near approach of an enemy four times our number and the disorganized condition of our men filled me with sorrow. Whilst the scenes of which I have given but an imperfect account were transpiring, one Brigade kept the enemy at bay about 1½ miles from Manassas. Between 6 and 7 o'clock orders were given to fall into ranks and to my great surprise the men obeyed with the utmost promptness.

Soon the disorganized mob assumed the appearance of a formidable army, each Brig. filing into their places in their respective divisions; and now displaying a sight as pleasing and formidable as its previous appearance was painful and discouraging.

Jackson's basic strategy now was to "keep Pope in play," to pin him down until the main body of Lee's army should arrive to deliver the finishing blow. At the same time the Confederate general had to protect his own force — greatly inferior in numbers to Pope's — from being annihilated. It was the case of a terrier with his teeth in the throat of an opponent four times his size and strength; the terrier would win if he could hold on; but without help he could not hold on for long.

(Night of 27–28) With this double purpose in view Jackson retreated in a northwest direction from Manassas Junction to a position around Groveton, six miles away, with his easternmost wing resting on Bull Run Creek. He was thus luring Pope closer to the spot where Longstreet was expected soon to arrive. And, in case the latter general did not come up in time, the location at Groveton afforded Jackson opportunity for a quick retreat toward Thoroughfare Gap.

Father Sheeran fully appreciated the situation:

Aug. 28   The truth is ... we were in a desperate condition. Pope was now with an army of some 80,000 [a rather exaggerated estimate; 70,000 would be closer to the truth] between us and our supplies [i.e., the stores carried by Lee's army]. Large Federal reinforcements were advancing against us from Washington and Alexandria. Thus we were between two powerful armies. But our men felt confident that Jackson knew his business and [they] gave themselves no concern.

In fact, Longstreet, on the 28th, was through Thoroughfare Gap, but was still 12 miles away, with the main body of Lee's force strung out behind him. Following his brigade to the Groveton area, the chaplain had some forebodings:

The army was in appearance once more demoralized. Having stacked arms some ran to the fortification (abandoned by us last year) in order to take a view of the surrounding country; some scattered themselves through Centerville [Groveton?] visiting former acquaintances; others seeking something to refresh the animal man, while the greater number, yielding to the demand of nature, sought fence corners, shade trees, etc. to repose their wearied frames.

Early on the next day (the 29th) Jackson's forces were being hardpressed. Longstreet was not yet on the scene. Characteristically, Stonewall fought his way out of the bag temporarily with a flanking thrust at the Federal left. When Pope countered with a powerful blow at the Confederate center, Jackson held him off for two hours and finally drove him back.

During these actions Father Sheeran was close behind the lines, serving a field hospital and having a few adventures himself:

Aug. 29   In passing along our lines, I met a few of our men who, as yet, had not caught up with the regiment since the battle of Bristow. I felt it my duty to rebuke them for their straggling propensities, for this was not the first time some of them had been absent from an engagement. But when I looked down and saw some of these poor fellows barefooted, I felt more disposed to pity than scold. . . .

Now [a few hours later] I discovered a general movement along our lines. Our Major told me it was no place for me, "I had better retire"; but I felt no alarm. Soon the orders were given to fall into ranks. I rode over the battlefield in front of our lines to see if I could recognize any of our dead. I was now in a dangerous position: between our lines and those of the enemy although I was not aware of it. For a moment our men were occupied, viewing the Yankee lines now visible, on a hill about three quarters of a mile distant. Soon however I saw our Division filing into line of battle and one of our battalions had taken position about two hundred yards to my right. Not dreaming of an immediate engagement, I was going up to the boys of the battery to speak a few words of encouragement, when suddenly all eyes were turned towards me or in the direction whence I came. It would appear that the Yankees took me for an officer for they evidently intended for me a shell that passed directly over my head, and burst some hundred yards in advance. I turned around and saw they had a battery in position on an opposite hill from which they immediately sent another fearful missile after me. I now looked upon a change of base as the most prudent strategy; and with a speed surpassing even any of Stonewall's flank movements I filed to the right and made for a woods some two hundred yards distant, in the meantime receiving friendly salutations from the generous Yankees.

"Where is Longstreet?" was the question being anxiously asked by the Confederates as Pope, later on August 29, attacked heavily again. Two incidents, however, witnessed by Father Sheeran, testified to the soundness of the corps' morale:

Aug. 29   Now occurred one of the most laughable incidents of the war. The Yankees had placed a mountain howitzer opposite the 15th La. Reg. which very much annoyed the boys. Having repelled the attack of the N. Y. infantry the gallant 15th boldly charged this battery which they captured with a large squad of Yankees. Desirous of securing their booty and the horses of the battery being killed, they harnessed the Yankees and compelled them to haul the artillery into our lines. The sight of some fifty Yankees hitched to a piece of artillery, with the 15th charging bayonets, coming across the battle-field at a double quick drew forth a burst of laughter from our Confederate boys. . . .

The 1st La. R. was out of ammunition and in fact nearly out of strength as they had been fighting for several hours against ten times their number. Col. Nolan* who commanded the 1st was expecting reinforcements every moment. To abandon his position on the bank of the R.R. would have turned the tide of victory against us. The gallant boys of the 1st were not

---

* Lieutenant-Colonel Michael Nolan, 1st (Nelligan's) Louisiana Infantry.

long in deciding what to do. Throwing down their empty guns they attacked and drove back the enemy with rocks which they found in abundance on the roadside. The other regiments as they got out of ammunition followed their example and soon it became a battle of rocks. It may appear strange, but it is nevertheless true that our men did as much execution with these new missiles of war as with their musket balls, for after the battle many of the Yankees were found on the field with broken skulls.

The critical moment at Second Manassas is succinctly described by Father Sheeran:

Aug. 29

Late after-noon

However this unequal contest could not long be continued. The enemy were advancing in still greater numbers, and without reinforcements our wearied men would have to fall back, and that would amount to their destruction. . . . It was now within an hour of night; our whole line was engaged since 3 P.M. in close combat with troops brought up fresh every hour. . . . But fortunately at this critical period our reinforcements came up in solid columns, their battle-flags in the face of the enemy. The object which Pope was trying to prevent was now accomplished. Longstreet had reached the plains of Manassas; Gen. Hood's* Div. which formed Longstreet's left came to Jackson's assistance.

Lee had executed a movement that Moltke has termed the supreme test of military genius — the bringing together of a commander's two armies at the precise moment in a field of battle.

Aug. 29

Late after-noon and evening

Thus our whole line extended and reinforced fell upon the enemy with savage ferocity. The shouts of our boys echoed on every side. The lines of the enemy broke, but were again rallied. Our boys saluted them with musketry

---

* Lieutenant General John Bell Hood, C.S.A.

and advanced on a charge. The enemy yielded with reluctance, and fought as they fell back. About half past 8 o'clock they retired in every direction being obliged to quit the field.

In the fierce contest the enemy acknowledged the loss of 8,000 but whoever surveyed the field of carnage as I did must conclude this estimate was far too low. The loss on our side was comparatively small. . . .

General Longstreet having formed a junction with Stonewall, Gen. Lee began to make arrangements for a general engagement [which, on the next day, he won].

Father Sheeran gives his usual generous estimate of the damage inflicted on the Federals in this battle:

Aug. 30   About half an hour before dark we heard the glad tidings that the Yankees were flying in every direction, the battle was fought and the victory won. The enemy was routed leaving behind some 8000 prisoners, about 20,000 or 22,000 killed and wounded, and an immense quantity of cannon and small arms, besides wagons and ambulances.

The diary now recounts some incidents of the aftermath of the Manassas fighting:

Aug. 29-30 When our men fell back to their old position on Friday night, Pope imagining we were retreating telegraphed to Washington that he had "whipped Jackson and had him in a bag." On the reception of this news some of the dignitaries of that *great* city repaired to Manassa [sic] with the expectation of seeing Stonewall and his "ragged Confederates." These were some eight in number, one half of whom were *ladies*. This excursion party was somewhat surprised when Gen. Stuart* paid them his

---

* Brigadier General James Ewell Brown Stuart, C.S.A.

compliments and informed them that they were his prisoners. The ladies were sent home, but the "gents" were reserved to grace our triumphal procession. They were obliged to accompany the darky prisoners during the march of some three or four days. Never did I see men so mortified as these Washington *gentry*. In truth they no doubt admired the negroes, but they appeared to have a terrible dislike for their company. During this night and next morning we succeeded in removing all our wounded to the hospital where they were all well cared for.

Sunday,
Aug. 31

I will not speak of my fatigue of the past night and previous day for they were nothing compared with that of our brave men who were fighting the battles of their country. I felt inclined to rest but this was impossible, as orders were given to remove all the wounded that could bear the change to Aldie and Middlebury. This occupied all day Sunday. In the afternoon I visited some other hospitals and prepared some of our Catholic soldiers for death. . . . Never did men accomplish more, suffer more, and complain less.

Sept. 1

This morning arose much refreshed and not being certain of the real destination of the Army, I resolved to visit the battlefield in order to see if all our men were taken off, or if any of the unfortunate enemy needed my services. O! may I never again witness such scenes as I saw this day. I passed over only that part of the battle field in front of Jackson's Corps, but the sights there were truly heartrending. Our Pioneers corps had been busy during Sunday morning burying our own dead, 500 in number, and in the afternoon those of the enemy. Yet on this morning the Yankees in front of the R.R. occupied by the La. troops were lying in heaps. Those in front of the R.R. had something of the appearance of men, for they were killed with rocks or musket balls and with their face to our men. But those scattered throughout the woods and over the fields presented a shocking spectacle. Some with their brains oozing out; some with the face shot off; others with their bowels protruding; others with shattered limbs. I think it would be no exaggeration to say that in front of Jackson's lines alone there were nearly 5,000 dead Yankees. Consider that some of these were four days unburied, some three, and the remainder two, and you can form an estimate of the loathsome scene. They were almost as black as negroes, bloated and some so decomposed as to be past recognition. And it was nearly impossible to bury them. Our men had removed most of the wounded under the shade of the woods and to the adjacent houses.

I visited some of these unfortunate men and found them in a deplorable condition. Many had been without food for three or four days and had no one to hand them as much as a drink. I gave them what assistance and encouragement I could. I met with some Catholics who were severely wounded, and endeavored to prepare them to meet their God.

On my return from the wounded I met the Head Surgeon of Pope's army coming with a flag of truce, to see after his wounded. He addressed himself to me in a tone of authority. "Where, sir, will I find our wounded?" "What wounded do you mean?" "Our wounded." "Do you mean the wounded prisoners?" The fellow did not want to acknowledge that they were prisoners. However I gave him no information until he admitted they were. I then showed him a distance of some four miles, and told him that, no matter where in that direction he might go, he would find his men.

He then very politely invited me to accompany him, but I politely declined, telling him my duties called me elsewhere. Before parting, however, I requested him as a matter of charity, justice and humanity to have some of his men detailed to bury their dead, which he promised to do.

I now turned my steps towards our wagon team, hoping to learn the whereabouts of our brigade.... Near our wagon train and in a ravine N. West of Sudley's ford, were about 700 negroes of all ages and sexes; besides there were 300 officers of Pope's command, and consequently not to be *paroled* with the Washington Gents who were magnanimous [enough] to come to see Jackson and the Rebel captives taken by Pope; or, as they said themselves, "to care for the wounded." Generous souls! I conversed freely with these officers and "gents." The former complained much of their condition; the scanty supply of food; and of being dragged about with negroes. I told them their condition as prisoners was to be attributed to their own voluntary act of engaging in such a cause, and their not being *paroled* was their misfortune of having served under a commander who disregarded all the laws of civilized warfare and divested himself of every feeling of humanity. As regards the want of provisions they had not legitimate cause of complaint, for their government did all they could to starve the people of the South by blockading our ports, ravaging the country, plundering the inhabitants, burning our towns, leaving thousands of our people homeless and hungry; and if they now suffered it was all their own fault. And as to their sable companions, I thought they ought to be delighted with them. Why should they complain of having to accompany those for the love of whom they were desolating the South and trying to exterminate its inhabitants?

One of the Yankee officers, a N. Yorker by no means pleased with my sympathy gave vent to his feelings and patriotism in the following strain: "I came to fight for the Union, to put down this rebellion, and I will fight till I die for the flag of my country!" I told him plainly that such talk was mere nonsense; there was *No Union* to fight for, nor was there a rebellion to put down, for the people of the South were merely defending their national and constitutional rights; but as regarded his fighting to death for the flag of his country no person could believe him to be sincere, for his present condition as a prisoner showed that he did not mean what he said. Some of the Washington gents requested me to intercede for their liberation, protesting that they came on an errand of mercy. I replied that I could not interfere in such matters, exhorting them to bear their captivity with patience as it would give them some idea of the miseries of a war they were carrying against innocent people.

Hearing reports of another engagement near Chantilly, seven miles north of Centerville, and knowing that he would be needed to attend to the wounded, Father Sheeran rode off to the new battlefield:

Sept. 2   I took the road from Sudley's Mills towards Middlebury until I came to Fairfax and Alexandria pike at which I turned to the right. I was accompanied by an old gentleman from La. named Miller and the father of our acting Adjutant who was killed* in the battle of Friday.

On this road we met many wagons loaded with provisions which the good people of the surrounding country were sending to our wounded soldiers. This unsolicited act showed how deeply interested the people

---

* The officer killed in action was probably Major M. B. Miller, of Louisiana.

were in the cause for which our patriots were fighting. We have travelled but a few miles on the Alexandria pike when sights anything but pleasant presented themselves. Nothing but stragglers was [sic] to be seen in every direction. The old gentleman, my companion, smarting under the loss of his son, felt indignant at seeing so many of our men fall behind and with difficulty could be kept from quarreling with them. He frequently cried shame at them and told them they were not worthy of belonging to the brave Confederate army of Manassas. My companion was becoming anything but agreeable, for, although his rebukes were well merited by some, yet by the greater number they were not deserved, as many of the fellows were broken down.

About 2 P.M. I reached our regiment at Chantilly, the homestead of Gen. Stuart, and heard from it the account of the engagement of the previous evening in which our regiment, now reduced to a skeleton, had lost two killed and twenty wounded. It was in this Battle that the Yankee, Gen. Kearney* and another Federal Gen. were killed. I was sorry to hear that in this engagement some of our regiments did not do as well as usual. About 5 o'clock on Mon. afternoon, we had just formed a line of battle with the 1st La. Brig. on our right and some Georgia regiments on our left and had sent out our skirmishers, when suddenly the Yankees concealed in the woods poured a heavy fire on our ranks. This fire our boys returned with their usual spirit and then began to advance on the enemy. Here some *Greenhorn,* acting as Adjutant, came running along our lines, crying out that the Yankees were advancing in three heavy columns and endeavoring to flank and turn our right. This information which should have been brought

---

* Brigadier General Philip Kearny, U.S.A. (Note misspelling by Father Sheeran.)

to the Gen. alone caused a panic among some of our regiments, for we had but a very small force present to oppose the enemy's advance. The Ga. regt. broke and retreated, nor could many of them be rallied notwithstanding the efforts of some of their brave officers. There were also two of the La. regiments that did not display their usual valor. But the 14th and the 5th La. manfully stood their ground, contending with the powerful columns of the enemy, and finally succeeded in driving them from the field. . . .

We captured 1,300 prisoners whom I afterwards saw parade. Having ascertained where our dead and wounded were, I had the former buried and latter removed to our hospital some two miles from the field of Battle. This night was spent to a late hour in ministering to the spiritual wants, as well as washing and dressing the wounds of those who had not as yet been sent back. My old friend, Mr. Miller, accompanied me and displayed the very best disposition to render all the assistance in his power. He was a Protestant and as such cared nothing about confession or any other sacrament. Yet he went around among the wounded inquiring particularly if any of them were Catholics and, if so, came and told me.

After thus ministering to the wounded and dead at Chantilly, Father Sheeran resumed his ride northward and rejoined his Brigade near the town of Dranesville. There was much speculation among the men as to where Jackson was leading them now. After passing through Leesburg on September 4 it was clear that they were to cross the Potomac. Now the secret was out:

Sept. 4   The long cherished dream of some of our editors and stay-at-home military men was about to be realized. Maryland was to be invaded. The greater number of our

men were enthusiastic, expecting that the Marylanders
would flock to our standard by thousands, and that thus
recruited we would carry the war into the enemy's
country, that we would soon unfurl our flag on the
banks of the Susquehanna. I must confess I did not
participate in these bright visions. I rather looked upon
it as an experiment the result of which was involved in
doubt.

On the next day, as the troops splash over the river into Maryland,
Father Sheeran comments briefly (Sept. 5): "I rode slowly across . . .
[and] offered my humble prayers to God that this expedition might
prove advantageous to the cause for which we were contending."

Lee had decided to invade Pennsylvania. But, before he could safely
do so, he must make his rear secure by the wiping out of the Federal
pockets at Martinsburg and Harpers Ferry. This latter task was assigned
to Jackson's corps. Lee took his main army up west of Hagerstown, and
waited for Jackson to do the mopping-up job. Father Sheeran traveled
northwest with old Stonewall:

Sept. 6   The numerous cornfields growing abundant crops;
               the well stocked pasture ground, the numerous and
               beautiful orchards whose trees were groaning under the
               weight of delicious fruit; the granaries and barnyards
               thronged with poultry and swine presented a pleasing
               contrast with the desolate fields and plundered habita-
               tions of North Eastern Virginia. Here evidently the peo-
               ple had only heard of the war, without having realized
               any of its sad ravages. During our march this morning
               the people flocked to the roads to see us. Among the
               crowds we saw some friendly countenances, but the
               greater number looked upon us with seeming
               indifference.

As he approaches the town of Frederick:

               These three miles were spent in rather serious reflec-
               tions. The surrounding country, the neighboring hills,

the distant Blue Ridge were all to me old acquaintances. My numerous trips over the Balt. & O. R.R., from Baltimore to Cumberland, the pleasant scenes of my college days, the once happy state of our country and its now distracted condition all presented themselves to my imagination. I grieved to think that a Union, which was once the political idol of my soul, was now shattered forever.

With causes and effects before my mind, how clearly did I perceive their close and intimate connection. "According to the order of ideas is the order of events" is the saying of a celebrated author and how true this is the recent history of our country clearly demonstrates. Some twenty years ago a few fanatics residing in New England began to preach in the name of liberty and humanity doctrines subversive of our social and political edifice. The name of *liberty* was used as a cloak for their disorganizing principles. They enkindled the fires of social and political discord, which soon spread over our once happy country, enveloping it in a general conflagration. Such was the order of ideas. Such the cause. The consequence is a war unjust, cruel, barbarous and inhuman, which has for its object the enforcing of these destroying principles.

These were the thoughts that occupied my mind during my brief journey from Monocasy bridge until I arrived at a toll-gate a short distance from Frederick. Here my meditations were interrupted by a "bit of a row." One of our men who had probably drunk *more* than was necessary was disputing with a lady at the toll-gate. She contended that he had taken bacon for which he had not paid, exclaiming at the same time that she was a *Unionist,* and must not be imposed on by any Confederate rebel. I investigated the matter. She found she was mistaken. I told her she should not be so uncharitable as to accuse any person of an act of dishonesty without undeniable proofs, but we would be willing to forgive her if she would give three cheers for Jeff Davis. This she refused to do, but we left her in better humor.

★   ★   ★

In taking a view of the Barracks [after arriving in Frederick] I met one of the Sisters of Charity who had charge of the Hospital.* I dismounted in order to speak to her but to my great surprise saw her appear very much embarrassed. I was not long in discovering the cause of it. I had on a Confederate uniform, and there were several Yankee Surgeons and officers on the gallery of the Barracks watching me closely. The poor Sister, no doubt, feared that she might be accused of giving information to the enemy, or showing sympathy for the rebels. Perceiving this, I mounted my horse, and unceremoniously cut short our acquaintance, and did not afterwards try to renew it. . . .

The questions of our boys reminded me that I should at least put on a clean shirt before going in the presence of civilized beings. I entered a Jew's clothing store in company with some of the boys who soon supplied me with a white shirt, handkerchief, and many other useful articles. The storekeeper being appraised of who I was, invited me to a room and furnished me with water, soap and a towel. Oh! that happy moment! A good wash and a clean shirt were luxuries I had not enjoyed for over three weeks. Feeling the importance of my new white and well-starched appendage I repaired to

---

* The Confederates encamp on the shores of the Monocacy, just outside the town. They will visit and revisit Frederick itself during their short stay in the area.

the house of the Jesuit Fathers [in Frederick] by whom I was kindly received. Here I had the pleasure of meeting Father Hubert* for the first time in four days. He was, like myself, disguised in Confederate *mud*. . . .

It was now about 4 P.M. and as there were some few hours of daylight yet I thought I would employ them in viewing the place. The city was crowded with soldiers who came to see and to purchase. Many of them had already disguised themselves in new shirts and some even wore gloves. The barber shop was taken by storm and the stores were full of liberal purchasers. The windows, doors, and balconies were filled with ladies who generally showed the most enthusiastic feelings. When we entered the town the Federal flag was still flying on the Market house and in a place very difficult of access; soon our boys tore down the Yankee bunting. When seeing this flag, now the emblem of tyranny torn in shreds amidst the shouts of assembled thousands, sorrowful reflections came to my mind. A few short years ago that very flag was the emblem of our national greatness and to defend it every Southern citizen would have sacrificed his life. But now that it had become the standard of tyranny and injustice, its fall elicited the enthusiasm of the Southern people. Such is the instability of all earthly things. Having seen the greater portion of this beautiful city I returned to the house of the Jesuit Frs. and having partaken of a good supper, retired early to rest. I was tired but could not compose a mind agitated by the reflections and scenes of the day. How strangely this night contrasted with those of the previous five weeks. From the time we left Camp Wheat for Cedar Mountain to our arrival near Frederick, scenes of blood, carnage, fatigue, hunger and thirst

---

* Confederate Chaplain Darius Hubert, attached to 1st (Nelligan's) Louisiana Infantry.

constantly presented themselves to me. I had seen hundreds of thousands of my fellowmen drawn up in battle array, heard the thundering of the artillery and felt the earth quake beneath its powerful voice. I had heard the loud shouts of victorious triumph, as well as the groans and lamentations of our wounded and dying. I had seen the worst passions of the human heart displayed under the names of *liberty* and *humanity*. I had seen displayed a patriotism more noble, more elevated, more brave and chivalrous than any recorded in the world's history.

But I found myself that night not on the wearying march, not in the tented camp, not on the gory field of battle, not in the hospital listening to the suppressed moans of bleeding patients. Oh! no! once more I found myself within the peaceful walls of a convent. Before me was the image of my crucified Savior, near me was that of His Immaculate Mother. These and other pious objects recalled to my mind my peaceful cell in New Orleans and, had I wings, quickly would I have flown to it, there to shelter myself at least for a time from the scenes of bloody strife, now desolating our country. These were the thoughts which revolved rapidly through my imagination until about 11 o'clock when the powers of body and mind yielding to the soothing influence of *Somnus* I thought no more of Mars.

Sept. 8   [In Frederick two days later] many of our officers now disguised in clean shirts, new boots, spurs, etc. displayed their equestrian skill, and attracted the attention, if not the laughter, of the fair ones on the galleries. Having ridden through the principal part of the town, we repaired [again] to the house of the Jesuit Fathers. The scene here was a most affecting one. The good Fr.

Ward,* Master of Novices, was busily occupied waiting on our poor soldiers as they passed to partake of refreshments which he had prepared abundantly for them. In fact he had an open house at all hours during the three days of our sojourn in Frederick. I had the pleasure of meeting here the Very Rev. Fr. Provincial of S.J.** and Rev. Fr. McGuire† of Washington who requested me to procure a pass for them to return to Baltimore.

In company with R. Fr. McGuire I next visited the convent of the Sisters of the Visitation, a splendid and spacious building directly opposite the Jesuit Novitiate. Here I found that the Srs. had refreshments in abundance prepared for our soldiers, the young ladies of the Academy being occupied from morning till night preparing food and waiting on our soldiers. The good Srs. received me very kindly, brought us through the various departments of the Academy, and invited us to partake of some refreshments prepared for the occasion. I was not a little surprised to hear the enthusiastic feelings displayed by these good Srs. for the success of the Southern cause. They assured me that whilst our brave men were fighting the battles of their country they and their children were praying for the success of our arms. Recrossing the street to the Jesuit Frs. I met the good Father Ward with some dozen canteens strung about his neck. "Father," said I, "in the name of common sense what are you doing with these canteens?" "Well," said he, "when I was out on the street I met some of your boys inquiring where they could get some molasses to buy, and I thought the poor fellows too tired to be running around, so I am going to the cellar to fill them." I could not help laughing at the picture the

* Father James A. Ward, S.J.
** Father A. M. Paresce, S.J.
† Father Sheeran's spelling is incorrect. The priest was Father Bernard A. Maguire, S.J.

good Father presented in the midst of the canteens. Though small, it was truly a noble act.

They leave Frederick and push northwest toward Martinsburg. At Williamsport, Father Sheeran has some sad memories:

Sept. 12   Whilst resting on my horse, near the bluffs of the Potomac, my eye caught a glimpse of the summit of Cove mountain some twenty miles distant. At the base of this picturesque mountain I had lived for some five years. With this spot were connected some of the dearest associations of my life, and ones that nature would hold in eternal recollection. For a moment I yielded to feelings of sadness, and sighed for the good associations [of] which God in His Providence had deprived me.

★   ★   ★

Sept. 13   [After a brief stop at Martinsburg, which Jackson found to be already evacuated by the Federals], we resumed our march this morning in the direction of Harpers Ferry. During this morning we frequently met some of our cavalry who went in quest of the Yankees, returning with squads of prisoners. There was one thing very remarkable about these unfortunate subjects of King Abe 1st; they were nearly all in their stocking feet. We did not know whether they were caught sleeping, or threw away their shoes in order to make better time on their "Back to Washington Stampede." On this occasion the generous feelings of many of our brave soldiers were displayed. Although these hirelings by their wholesale acts of plunder, and by their barbarous treatment of the people of the Valley had sacrificed every claim to human sympathy, yet our boys thinking our cavalry had stripped them of their shoes, freely denounced this act. (We were afterwards informed that they were captured in a shoeless condition.)

[The siege and capture of Harpers Ferry was effected quickly.]

Sept. 15   My first visit [after the surrender] was to a cemetery where a detachment of Yankees were burying their companions, killed in the morning's engagement. In my conversation with these men I found many of them were Catholics. These misguided, poor fellows on finding out who I was, were rejoiced to see me and seemed to forget for the moment that they were in the hands of the enemy. I conversed long and freely with them, disabusing their minds of many wrong ideas they had entertained with regard to the war and the people of the South.

Meanwhile Lee, with his army spread out around Hagerstown, was becoming anxious. He had expected Jackson to join him sooner, and was increasingly apprehensive of a Federal attack at Turners Gap, in South Mountain, about ten miles southeast of Hagerstown and about the same distance east of Sharpsburg. McClellan struck at South Mountain before Lee could sufficiently strengthen the position and the Confederate forces converged toward Sharpsburg to make a stand there. "Where is Jackson?" the Confederate men in the ranks were grumbling. An observation of Father Sheeran as he rode north from Harpers Ferry with Hill's division may provide a regrettable reason for Jackson's delay:

Sept. 17   Having spent a short time here [at Harpers Ferry] I resumed my journey. The scenes I witnessed this day were the most painful of the war. The country was literally crowded with stragglers. I presume that more than one half of Hill's* Division had fallen out of the ranks during the march from Harpers Ferry to Shepherdstown, and I presume an equal proportion of the Divisions preceding it. Some of these men excited my sympathy, for they looked sick and broken-down but

---

* Major General Ambrose P. Hill, C.S.A.

others again I looked upon with contempt, for they evidently were professional stragglers. Some of them even threw their guns in the fence corners. I am sorry to say that these stragglers were largely represented by officers. These facts came under my own observation.

Father Sheeran did not come up in time to witness the battle of Sharpsburg [Antietam]. It was one of the bloodiest engagements of the war, and a decisive Confederate defeat. The patriotic Father Sheeran did not, at the time, admit these facts. "The lying dispatches of McClellan notwithstanding," he says, *"the victory was ours."* But it is McClellan, not Father Sheeran, who has history on his side. A further remark of the chaplain, however, deserves careful consideration:

Sept. 18   I have already spoken of the stragglers from our army during this battle on whom rests the responsibility of prolonging this barbarous war. Had they been at their post that day, the Yankees under McClellan could have been exterminated, or had Gen. Lee 5,000 fresh troops on the following day he would have utterly routed the enemy.

Whatever the recriminations and interpretations, Lee's invasion of Pennsylvania was halted — for that year — and the Army of Northern Virginia withdrew southward. Shortly afterward Father Sheeran received permission for a leave of absence *ad libitum* (its duration to be at his discretion) and departed for Richmond.

A lesser clash, with its own drama, is said to have occurred some time (date unspecified) during the campaign just completed. Because of what it reveals of Father Sheeran's character it is worth recording.* A fair judge would probably be forced to admit that the chaplain's zeal — undoubtedly sincere and selfless — sometimes led him to indiscretions:

Going to his tent one day, General Jackson sternly rebuked the priest for disobeying his orders, and re-

---

* The source for this (presumed) incident is: Rev. Joseph Flynn, *The Story of a Parish* [The Church of the Assumption, Morristown, N. J., of which Father Sheeran was pastor after the war] (New York: The Columbia Press, 1892), p. 111. It must be admitted that the authenticity of the happening is suspect, although, given the character of the chaplain and that of the general, the exchange of words might have occurred.

proached him with doing what he would not tolerate in any officer of his command. [The offense was apparently one of interference with military administration.] "Father Sheeran," said the General, "you ask more favors and take more privileges than any officer in the army." "General Jackson," said Fr. Sheeran, "I want you to understand that as a priest of God I outrank every officer in your command. I even outrank you, and when it is a question of duty I shall go wherever called." The General looked with undisguised astonishment on the bold priest and without replying left his tent.

After resting at the Confederate capital (Sept. 27 ff.) for ten days and "procuring some necessary supplies for another campaign," Father Sheeran on October 10 rejoined his regiment now stationed twelve miles below Winchester. Although he did not realize the fact, he was beginning with them the campaign that would culminate at the fierce battle of Fredericksburg, December 13, 1862. As the chaplain himself explained the situation: "Since the battle of Sharpsburg, McClellan was marshalling his forces on the Maryland side of the Potomac. The Washington authorities were forcing him to advance. He had possession of Harpers Ferry, and from there he made a reconnaissance in force, feeling for General Lee. . . . His subsequent movements showed that he resolved to cut off our retreat to Richmond."

Lee, therefore, determined to march south toward Culpeper and then, moving eastward toward the Rappahannock, cover his capital and save his army. For a while, however, the Confederate commander held his army in the vicinity of Winchester, waiting for McClellan to make the first move southwest.* Father Sheeran was favorably impressed by the condition of the Confederate forces:

Oct. 18   In three months I had not seen the army in such a good condition as this morning. The stragglers and those broken down were all up with their commands; besides many had returned from the hospitals, recovered from their wounds. We had also received many

---

* On November 5 McClellan will be replaced by Maj. Gen. Ambrose E. Burnside.

conscripts. The boys were in the best of spirits and resolved to make the Yankees lament the day they followed them over the Potomac.

During this comparative lull in military operations, Father Sheeran had some opportunities to display his firmness of character:

Sunday, [While the regiment was encamped at Bunker's Hill,
Oct. 26 near Winchester] . . . I received a visit from an Irishman named Pennyman. He was the son of a distinguished pedagogue, and consequently prided himself on his knowledge of mathematics; besides, he was a Union man, "dyed in the wool." He endeavored to convince me by a mathematical demonstration that the North was right and would conquer the South. After showing him that the North had no right to force the South to remain in the Union as England had no right to force Ireland into a union with her I added: "Now, sir, I will tell you what I think your duty as a good citizen requires. Obey the laws of your adopted State, Virginia, which has afforded you for many years the protection of her laws, and under them you have acquired property and a domicile. She above all other states has a reserved right to leave the Federal compact. She has done so and for motives of public good formed a league with her sister states of the South. You are bound in conscience to obey her just laws and respect her authority. But should you not feel disposed to take this advice, then my next best one is that you should take a trip to the North and never come back."

★   ★   ★

Sunday, [On another occasion while in camp all day in "an
Nov. 9 oak forest"], some stowed themselves in retired places to indulge in their favorite propensity of gambling.

Seeing the evils resulting from this vice I had prohibited it in camp. The boys, knowing this, used to hide in order to enjoy this stolen sport. This Sunday afternoon, knowing that I was absent from camp, they played their game publicly and for stakes of one hundred and fifty dollars. Anxious to know how things were going on, late in the afternoon I visited the camp and saw a number of the boys surrounding some object that seemed to attract their attention. Unobserved I advanced to the crowd and looking over some of their shoulders I beheld two groups with cards in hand and countenances very serious. Between them was a pile of bills containing the above amount. By this time I was observed by all around, but not by the card players who were too much engrossed with their stake to notice anything else. Slowly I bent forward until within reach of the money, when by a well directed grasp I secured some $60 of the stakes besides a part of two other bills. The gamblers, not knowing who was there, made use of a very rough exclamation, but finding out who it was took to their heels amid the shouts and laughter of the whole camp. This money I afterwards gave to the orphans of St. Joseph in Richmond.

Nov. 13   [Yet, Father Sheeran's sternness with the men did not apparently lessen their liking for him nor their desire to look out for his interests:] This day [at Winchester] Mr. Hassett* was near getting into a scrape on account of my horse now known by almost every soldier of our army as well as those of the enemy. With my permission, Mr. Hassett rode my horse out on some business, but when passing through Main St. Surgeon White** of our

---

* This gentleman evades identification. He was evidently a civilian on fairly intimate terms with Father Sheeran.

** There is no Doctor or Surgeon White listed as belonging to the 14th Louisiana Regiment. See footnote on p. 4 *supra.*

regiment halted him and demanded where he got that horse, saying it belonged to Father Sheeran. Mr. Hassett soon satisfied him that he did not steal it, as I was staying at his house. The explanation satisfied the Dr. and he allowed him to pass on.

On November 26 the Regiment learns that Jackson has gone ahead of Lee and is already at Gordonsville and swinging eastward toward Fredericksburg, to head off Burnside's* southward drive. Lee is following rapidly to join forces with Stonewall. On December 13 the two armies clashed at Fredericksburg and Burnside was stopped in his tracks, with fearful slaughter. After doing his duty with the wounded and dying, Father Sheeran continues his zeal for the morale of the army:

Dec. 16   About 8 o'clock this morning an officer came over from the regiment and informed me that Capt. V—— had disgraced himself and the regiment by his cowardice and that the men publicly denounced him. Knowing since my trip to Richmond that this captain had no commission in the regiment, I resolved to inform him of the fact and request him to withdraw from the command. It was a painful duty, but I did not want the brave 14th to be disgraced or demoralized. With difficulty I mounted my horse and rode over the battlefield where our men were yet under arms. I received many warm salutations from the boys as I passed along the line.

Coming up to the captain I called him aside and informed him that whilst in Richmond I ascertained that he had no official connection with the regiment, and suggested to him that he was of course free to throw up his command. He complained that he was badly treated by the department and he would see about it. When I observed that he did not act on my suggestion, I told

---

* Major General Ambrose Everett Burnside, U.S.A., was appointed to succeed McClellan on Nov. 5.

him that his own self-respect required that he should withdraw from the regiment because the boys accused him of being a coward. He remarked that he knew there were some who did not like him and, of course, they might make such charges. I told him that he was mistaken for it was not only a few who accused him of cowardice, but every man in the regiment. This was more than he could stand, so he rode off and notified the Brigade commander of his withdrawal, and the 14th got rid of the biggest coward that ever played soldier.

Learning that the Yankees were moving down on the other side of the river toward Port Royal, Jackson's corps took up its march in the same direction:

Dec. 20   On the way . . . we heard that one of the 8th La. had been frozen to death the night before whilst in a state of intoxication. We happened to meet three men sitting round a miserable fire. I stopped to see who they were. One of them attempted to come over to where I was standing, but fell on the way. I soon discovered that they were drunk and had a canteen full of whiskey. I shuddered when thinking of the condition of these miserable men. They were now hardly able to take care of themselves and I was satisfied if they should drink any more they would be frozen, for it was the coldest day of the season.

I rode up to them, had a kind "how d'ye do" and hearty shake hands. They all knew me very well. Standing round my horse, they were about to help themselves to a little more liquor. I very seriously asked the fellow with the canteen if he would let me have a little of the whiskey as I felt quite cold. He looked at me with an eye of suspicion and said "Will you promise not to spill it?" I pledged my word that I would not. He then with

somewhat of reluctance handed me the canteen. I threw
the canteen strap round my neck, and gave spurs to my
horse. The fellow made a grasp at my bridle but my
grey was too quick and soon sprang out of the way some
nine or ten rods. They were first disposed to be angry,
but seeing they could not get it back, began to laugh
right heartily. I advised them to follow their regiment
to camp and to be there when I came back.

★   ★   ★

Thursday,   Having heard some intimations that the boys were
Christmas   about to make me a Christmas present, I took occasion
to inform them that I did not stand in need of it but
if they wanted to honor our Infant Savior they might
bestow their charitable gifts to his representatives, the
poor orphans of St. Joseph's Asylum in Richmond. They
acted on my suggestion and during the following week
made up among themselves a very handsome sum of
$1,206.

1863

From the end of December, 1862, to the last week of March, 1863, Father Sheeran was again on leave in Richmond. Most of his time there he spent in ministering to the victims of the smallpox epidemic that was ravaging the city. On March 24 he was again with his regiment, then encamped at Guiney's Station near Fredericksburg. A few days later he had a consoling experience:

April 5   Today, Easter Sunday, is one which I shall ever remember on account of a few remarkable circumstances. The snow had been falling all night and early in the morning it continued to come down so thickly that one could hardly see fifty yards distant. I was somewhat sad at the prospect this morning presented. Anticipating pleasant weather we expected to celebrate Easter in a joyful manner. We were to have Mass at 8 A.M. and a large number of the Catholics of the brigade were prepared to go to Communion, but now what was to be done? But to my surprise I found a large concourse of boys around my tent. To see so many of our brave soldiers knee-deep in the snow, cheerfully awaiting the offering of the Holy Sacrifice of the Mass, was perhaps one of the most consoling sights of my life, and never did I pray more fervently for my congregation than on this occasion. But if it was edifying to see them standing in the snow before Mass commenced, how much more so to see them on their bended knees and with uncovered heads defying as it were the angry elements during the offering of the Holy Sacrifice. The

greater number of those present received Holy Communion, after which we recited the rosary of our Blessed
Mother as a part of our thanksgiving. My sermon this
day was necessarily short as I did not wish to detain
the poor men in the cold. I announced that I was to
leave camp on the following day in order to visit the
other portions of Gen. Lee's army and give the Catholic
soldiers belonging to it an opportunity of making their
Easter Communion.

Father Sheeran is making the most of the opportunity for improving
the men's morals:

April 24   This morning was cloudy and threatened rain. We
had Mass at 7 A.M. Nearly all the Protestants in camp
were present. I was much edified at the number of
Communions this day. As I ascended a little platform
erected for the occasion, it began to rain. This was rather
discouraging, but I resolved to preach "hail or shine."
This, however, I soon found no very easy matter, for
as the audience was very large and the wind and rain
were blowing in my face, I had to make more than an
ordinary effort to cause myself to be understood. In
this sermon I denounced blasphemy in the strongest
terms, and was much gratified that my remarks had
such a good effect upon all. During my short sojourn
in camp I heard the name of God scarcely once used
in a profane manner and many of the Protestants expressed a strong desire to have me return soon.

Sunday,   I heard many confessions this morning, had Mass at
April 26   10 A.M. and a very large congregation. Seeing so many
Protestants I thought it well before commencing to
make a few remarks explanatory of the Sacrifice of the
Mass. This I did as I intended to preach after Mass
on another subject. I was listened to with much attention. My sermon was on Mortal Sin and lasted for one
hour and a half. This was the longest sermon I had

ever preached, although it appeared to me about the shortest. The people listened with much patience and, I hope, profit. Father Smulders* preached at six o'clock to a large congregation on the subject of Hell.

[It almost seemed as if a spirit of Christian charity — sufficiently cautious — had temporarily seized at least some of the combatants:] Our picket line here extended some three miles along the river. At various places along this line our boys were amusing themselves by sending across the river their little schooner, laden with tobacco and other commodities to the Yankee pickets who lined the banks of the Rappahannock, receiving in exchange Yankee papers, coffee etc. I sent a note over in one of our little schooners, enquiring if there were any Catholic Chaplains in Hooker's army, and received from a Yankee Colonel an affirmative answer. I was much amused and indeed not a little surprised at the nautical skill displayed by our men in the construction, rigging and managing of their little craft. By a skillful setting of the sails and rudders they could, notwithstanding the rapidity of the current, cause their frail barks to make any point on the opposite shore. The Yankees did not appear to understand this business so well, for very few of their vessels came back so successfully as they went over, our boys having sometimes to swim in after their ships and carry them.

Now occurred what was perhaps Father Sheeran's most important interview of the whole war:

April 28   It was now evident from all indications that the whole army would soon be in motion [heading for the battlefield of Chancellorsville, although Father Sheeran was ignorant of the fact]. I was somewhat embarrassed to

---

* Father Aegidius Smulders, also a Redemptorist. At the outbreak of the war he had been stationed with Father Sheeran at New Orleans, and had also volunteered as a chaplain.

know what to do. I was some twelve miles from my regiment, my horse was in Richmond without which it would be impossible for me to follow the army, and to go to Richmond I could not without a pass which would require some two days to obtain according to the regular routine. I had often thought of visiting General Lee and asking him for a general pass to relieve me from the usual delays and trouble of obtaining one whenever I wished to leave camp. So after Mass the Father [Smulders] and I started for Gen. Lee's Headquarters.

We first repaired to the Adjutant General's office to make known the object of our visit. This officer told us that we could not obtain such a pass as I desired, and that the General was so busily occupied that he could not see us. I told him that I should have the pass, and I knew the General would not refuse it. The Adjutant with evident reluctance went to the General's tent and in a few moments came back and told us that Lee was prepared to receive us.

We entered his tent. The General received us standing, and then kindly invited us to a seat. "Well, gentlemen, what is your business?" he inquired. I stated our business. He told us that he did not know us, that we should come with the recommendation of our brigades' commanders. I told him that it was to avoid this old and troublesome routine of getting a pass that induced us to come to him personally, that we asked no favors for ourselves, and that we merely wished to make ourselves more efficient to the whole army by removing unnecessary causes of delay.

The General remarked: — "You are like other officers in the army and should not expect privileges which they cannot have." I now became a little warm at the unexpected refusal. "General, you say you do not know me. I have been with you in all your campaigns. I have been present at every battle fought by your army. I have never been absent from my duty. There are few officers in your army who do not know me and I am surprised, General, that you do not." For a few moments there was silence. The General at last addressed me. "Sir, it is just now I recognize you. Had I known you when you first came in you should have had no trouble. I now remember you well. Now tell me what you want, and I will do anything I can for you." "General, I merely want a pass to visit any portion of the army or any of the hospitals when I think my duty requires me to do so." He then wrote me a pass with his own hand which will last me to the end of the war if I should last so long. Having handed me mine, he asked me if my companion wanted one like it. He then wrote one for Father Smulders. Having obtained the long wished for pass we mounted our horses and rode to camp.

The battle of Chancellorsville (May 3–5) was Lee's first resounding victory as, in that spring of 1863, he turned on the Federal invasion force — now commanded by Hooker who had taken over command from Burnside after Fredericksburg — and badly mangled it. Basically, the Confederate tactic was a repetition of Second Manassas. Lee held Hooker fast while Jackson executed another dazzling end sweep and came up behind the Federals. Father Sheeran could not forget the scene of the battlefield when the fight was over:

May 6   I have passed over many a battlefield but this perhaps was the most revolting scene I had ever witnessed. Our line of battle extended over some eight miles and for that distance you see the dead bodies of the enemy lying in every direction, some with their heads shot off, some with their brains oozing out, some pierced through the head with musket balls, some with their noses shot away, some with their mouths smashed, some wounded in the neck, some with broken arms or legs, some shot through the breast and some cut in two with shells. But what was most shocking of all: the underbrush on one part of the battlefield took fire and for nearly half a mile burned the dead bodies and many of the wounded to a crisp.

During and after the engagement he had busied himself with the casualties, and had even extended his attention to the Yankee wounded and dying:

May 4   Across the road from our hospital was one full of Yankees. As usual having attended to the wants of our own men I visited the wounded of the enemy and offered my services. I found a good number of Catholics, some of whom were severely wounded. Having administered the sacraments to some I enquired if they had no surgeon of their own or any person to dress their wounds. They told me that they had several surgeons over there (pointing to an adjacent building), but they had paid no attention to them, did not even come to see them. I repaired to the house, enquired for the surgeons, told them of the painful condition of the wounded and requested them as a matter of humanity not to neglect them so, adding that we had now as much as we could do with our own wounded. They told me that they had no bandages to dress the wounds, no instruments to operate with, and that they were fatigued from the labors of the night. I remarked it would be some consolation to their wounded, if they would but visit them and wash the wounds of those who were bathed in their own blood. I next went to their men paroled to attend the wounded, asked why they did not wait on their companions, many of whom were suffering for a drink of water. They told me that they had no one to direct them, that their surgeons seemed to take no interest in the men.

I became somewhat indignant to hear the excuses of these worthless nurses, and putting on an air of authority ordered them to go to the rifle pits filled with the dead bodies of their companions and they would find hundreds of knapsacks filled with shirts, handkerchiefs and other articles that would make excellent bandages. They obeyed my orders with the utmost alacrity and soon returned with their arms full of excellent bandage material, and bringing them to me asked: "Now, sir, what shall we do with them?" "Go and tell your surgeons that you have bandages enough now." Off they went to the surgeons and I to our hospital. In about two hours I returned and was pleased to find the surgeons and nurses all at work attending to their wounded.

After Chancellorsville, Hooker pulled back his forces, and Lee soon followed him northward. The Confederate invasion of the north — which would end a month later at Gettysburg — was under way. But a sober analyst would have placed a high importance on a factor that probably was not fully appreciated at the time: the death of Jackson at Chancellorsville had deprived Lee of an almost indispensable lieutenant.

As he rode northward with the army, Father Sheeran had much with which to be pleased. His exhortations against gambling had resulted in a switch of the soldiers' attentions to the much less dangerous game of quoits. At a review of Early's and Johnson's divisions he had been publicly greeted by Lee:

May 27   There were many other Chaplains standing in the
Camp at   rear of the General's colors where we had a view of the
Hamilton's whole field. I carefully avoided looking at the General
Crossing, a lest he or others might think that I was seeking a
few hours' salutation from him. But he did not allow me to escape
horseback   his notice and extended his hand in a most cordial and

*ride from
Richmond* friendly manner. This mark of respect and friendship attracted universal attention, for I was the only one of all the Chaplains that he seemed to notice.

He was acquiring a rather close intimacy with General Ewell:

June 13   According to previous orders all were on the way at 4 o'clock and making towards Winchester. This was the first time I had seen General Ewell since he had his leg amputated.* He jestingly said, "Why, Father, you have your grey horse yet." I answered, "Yes, General, we are now becoming old companions." In the course of a brief conversation he requested me to pray that God might bless our efforts in the impending struggles. Not wishing to occupy much of his time I bade him good morning, and rode to my regiment now in the front of the column. Having marched some 5 miles we came to a halt.

June 16   When on my way towards Winchester I heard a voice calling me by the familiar name, Father Sheeran! On turning around I found it was General Ewell's Adjutant. He told me the General wished to see me and I of course dismounted and approached the General who received me with a warm handshake. Having taken me aside he told me he was anxious to see me in order that I might communicate to the Louisiana soldiers, officers and men his acknowledgment of the daring courage displayed by them in storming and capturing the enemy's breastworks. He said, next to God he was indebted to them for the almost bloodless victory he [had] achieved over Millroy. He then asked me as a favor that I would repair to Winchester and there take

---

* The general had suffered the loss of his leg as a result of having had it badly wounded at the battle of Groveton. In order to ride horseback he now had to be lifted to the saddle and strapped there.

charge of the wounded, giving me full authority to use
the sutlers' stores captured and all others which I might
think necessary for the comfort of the wounded heroes.

Having heard what the General had to say I hastened
to the hospital of the 1st Louisiana Brigade where I
visited all the wounded and then repaired to Winchester
to make permanent arrangements for them.

The chaplain's diary notation for June 16 was, "This afternoon I heard
that our whole army was on the way for Maryland." A week later he
is commenting on cultural divergencies between the Virginians and the
inhabitants of the Free State:

Passing through Hagerstown we were warmly received
by what appeared to be the most respectable portion of
the population, but evidently the majority of the inhabitants had no sympathy with us.

June 24   This morning we commenced our march in the direction of Chambersburg, passing through Middletown
formerly called Smoketown. I was sensibly struck by
the difference between the people of this part of the
country and the inhabitants of Virginia. Here you find
none of that grace of manners, high-toned sentiment,
or intellectual culture that you find in old Virginia.
Indeed, with all their wealth they appear little advanced
in civilization.

He stayed with Ewell's corps as it made its great arc into southern
Pennsylvania, through Chambersburg and Carlisle and — finally — on to
Gettysburg. He is proud of the way in which the Confederate troops
behaved as they passed through the enemy's country:

June 27   We marched to within 3 miles of Carlisle and camped
for the night. It was remarkable to see how orderly
our men conducted themselves on this march. It is true
many of them helped themselves to poultry, vegetables,
milk, etc., but I saw no wanton destruction of private

property. This I think redounds more to the honor of our army than a dozen victories over the enemy on the battlefield.

I perceived the people of this country were most agreeably disappointed. Knowing what their army had done to us; that they had burned our towns, laid waste our lands, driven helpless women and children from their homes, destroyed our implements of husbandry, that we might not be able to cultivate our lands, they very naturally expected that our soldiers would treat them in a similar manner. Great then was their surprise when they saw the conduct of our men. Many of these people told me that by our kindness and good treatment of the people we had made many friends among them.

He was at the battle of Gettysburg, at his post in a stone house on the battlefield itself, with the wounded. While his account of the engagement adds little to the other voluminous reports of the conflict, he makes an observation of some importance regarding what was possibly a tactical error of Lee:

July 3   We now discover but too late that our line of battle is too extended, being some six miles, and consequently we were without reserves where they were most needed. At every charge our men drove the enemy from their guns, but for want of sufficient support were unable to keep them. The enemy on the contrary had their lines contracted, and their army concentrated so that they could throw a powerful force on any point and very quickly. By this arrangement of the enemy's forces they suffered, it is true, terribly from the shells of our batteries, but they were enabled to throw an immense force on any advance of our weak, because too extended, lines. General Lee seeming now to despair of carrying

Father Sheeran's imitation-brown-velour-bound *Journals* as he carried them through his campaigns.

other of your men will take him; so I
prefer that you should keep him."

M. France sergeant got a horse by
being honest through necessity.

July 4th

About 2. A. M. as anticipated, we received
orders to move our hospital to a house
or rather barn some five miles from
the battle field on the Fairfax road
or the road marked F. At 3 we commenced moving off, leaving behind us
the most of our wounded with surgeons
and nurses to take care of them.

It was necessary to make this movement as quietly and cautiously as
possible, and before daylight, for
we had to pass from our left under
the range of the enemy's guns, and in
full view, if they had light to see us.
We were all full of anxiety lest
the dawn of day might expose us to
their view. Fortunately when day came
we were out of all danger, being beyond the range of their guns.

Specimen page of the *Journals:* account ⟨of⟩
his experiences at the battle of Gettysbur⟨g⟩

the Peninsula. The Battles of Williamsburg and Seven Pines, as also the Battles of Richmond were not transmitted, nor did I take any notes of them, although I passed through all these trying and direful scenes.

It here, however, our Regt. the 14th La. was transferred to Jackson's Command and knowing the enterprising character of our new Commander, I resolved to keep a journal in order that I might hereafter have a connected idea of the events through which we might pass. The following manuscript contains that journal, and as it was intended, not for public use but for our own community, I ask again as a favor, that should it fall into the hands of any stranger it may be destroyed.

Revd. Jas. Sheeran.
Chapln 14th La. Regt.

From Father Sheeran's Preface to his *Journals*: statement of his reasons for writing the *Journals*.

Front cover of Father Sheeran's "Holograp
Autobiography" written during his novicesh
with the Redemptorists. According to tl
Redemptorist custom, each novice was asked
write a brief account of his life up to the tin
of his entrance into the Congregation wit
special emphasis on the reasons why he ha
wished to become a Redemptorist priest.

the enemy's works reforms and contracts his line. His left is drawn in and his right and centre made more compact. In this position he defies the enemy to come out of his works and try the fate of a fair and open battle.

He recounts an incident involving the Confederate wagon train as, with its captured Federal spoils, it approaches the Potomac:

July 3   Here [approaching Williamsport] our quartermasters showed they were soldiers as well as financiers and resolved that the enemy should not obtain their coveted price. They brought the train to a halt and with the guns in the ordnance wagons armed their drivers, many of whom mounted on horses and mules acted with the cavalry, while the dismounted drivers acted with the sharpshooters. Our artillery open on the enemy with telling effect, while our cavalry and drivers charge them with a tremendous yell. The Yankees fly in every direction, leaving many fine horses behind. Our drivers fought like heroes. It is said to be a most laughable sight to see them mounted on their mules and in full pursuit of the flying enemy.

That the morale of the Confederate men in the ranks was not totally shattered at Gettysburg is evidenced by one of the most striking incidents of the retreat reported by the chaplain:

July 4   At length [as Father Sheeran is riding along on his horse with the retiring troops] the loud laughter of the men, comprising the head of A. P. Hill's column, advancing, banished every inclination to sleep. [At the moment, he has just told us, the chaplain is actually slumbering on his horse.] How agreeably did these men disappoint me! They had fought hard at Gettysburg, but failed to drive the enemy from their stronghold, and were now falling back and wading to their knees in mud and mire. These circumstances, calculated to depress the spirits of even the bravest men, had no such effect on these Confederate heroes. They were as cheerful a body of men as I ever saw; and to hear them, you would think they were going to a party of pleasure instead of retreating from a hard fought battle.

During the following four months Father Sheeran had a better opportunity to foster the religious life of the troops, not to mention the correction of their moral faults. The army was withdrawing slowly toward Richmond, while engaging in occasional clashes of the nature of rear-guard actions. There were, however, for the army no heavy military involvements; and Father Sheeran was able to exercise himself in more specifically priestly work for the men.

He had declared that he was "no respecter of persons." This quality he certainly displayed during this period:

Aug. 15

In camp, "only about four hundred yards from the old mansion of President Madison ... Mt. Pellier," near Orange Court House

I spoke today of the misconduct of some of our men whilst on picket, denounced their actions and informed the regiment that I could no longer, with any regard for my reputation as a priest, remain associated with such men. Many came to me after Mass and expressed their sorrow that I was about to leave them. Said I should not punish the whole regiment for the misconduct of a few.

Sunday, Aug. 16

We had Mass this morning at 7½, a large congregation and some communions. A short instruction after Mass. There was a regimental inspection of arms at

10 a.m. after which I had all the commissioned officers of the regiment assembled at my quarters. I called them all, Catholics as well as Protestants, that I might as much as possible avoid personalities in the remarks I was about to make.

I endeavored to impress upon their minds the importance of their positions as commissioned officers, as gentlemen and as Christians. I reminded them that if they had no regard for their own rank and position, they could not expect their men to respect them; nor would it be in my power to persuade them to do so. That, if they would violate the general principles of morality by conduct unbecoming gentlemen, no gentleman would like to associate with them. That, as Christians, if they violated the law of God, they would draw down, not the blessings, but the curse of God upon their own heads.

I expressed my sorrow to have to state that some of them by their recent conduct sacrificed all claims to the respect of a commissioned officer, a gentleman or Christian, and of course they must expect to suffer the consequences of their own acts. That henceforth those who knew themselves guilty of the imputed crimes would please to ignore me, as I would never recognize them even as acquaintances or friends until their improved conduct would satisfy me of their repentance.

In conclusion I reminded them they were responsible to God for all their actions and that they must one day render him an account for them. That as Confederate officers their country had claims upon them which they were bound to discharge. That as members of society they were bound to bring no disgrace upon their families by their misconduct. Thanking them all for their kind treatment of, and universal respect for me, and assuring them that nothing but a sense of duty compelled me to speak to them as I did, I permitted them to return to their quarters.

I was truly edified to see the respectful manner in which all listened to my remarks, and I am sure that the greater number of them turned them to advantage.

Notwithstanding what I had said to those officers whose conduct I had rebuked, one of them came to me today under the pretense of making an apology. His apology amounted to a gross insult which I indignantly resented, ordering him by his proper name to go to his quarters. He is heard by Colonel Zable* who takes no notice of him.

I visited General Ewell this afternoon for the purpose of informing him of this officer's conduct. The General is not at his quarters, but his Chaplain and staff received me kindly. Mr. Lacy** the Chaplain introduced himself to me saying he was very glad to see me, and invited me to a seat. The Reverend Gentleman very modestly loaded me with praises. Told me what he had heard of my efficiency on the battlefield, my attention to my men, my success in controlling them, and the high estimation in which I was held by the Generals of the army, how much my brother chaplains spoke of my energy and attention to business, how the Protestant bishop of Richmond† eulogized me etc. This certainly was soft soap enough for any one time.

Aug. 23   Father Hubert says Mass this morning at 7 and I at

---

* Lieutenant-Colonel David Zable, 14th Louisiana Infantry.
** The Reverend B. Tucker Lacy.
† Bishop John Johns, the Protestant Episcopal bishop of Virginia.

8½. As I had extended an invitation to the whole Brigade, both Protestants and Catholics, I had a large congregation.

It was my intention when giving the invitation to denounce in my sermon the vice of impurity. I felt it my duty to denounce this vice, to show how offensive it is to God, how degrading to our nature and how injurious in its moral and physical consequences. Some of the officers present thought the sermon was intended for them and indeed they thought right, but I intended that all my audience should profit by it. A filthy wretch whose crimes made him believe my remarks were personal, resolved to be avenged and consequently made charges against me without a word of comment [from his victim]. The result of the charges was that the author subjected himself to be cashiered from our regiment if he had not voluntarily resigned. I was much consoled to see the effects of this sermon on both officers and men.

Aug. 27   After Mass I complained of the cold indifference of the Catholics of the battalion. Told them I should return no more, but extend my labors to other commands where they would be more appreciated. They have a mass meeting, make an apology for the non-attendance this morning and beg me to remain with them another day as many of them were anxious to make their confession.

I found my remarks had their desired effect, so I agreed to remain until the next day. During the afternoon I heard many confessions, among them the confessions of two converts, one of whom I baptized the following morning.

Sunday,   The General* is a very profane man and I had often
Aug. 30   wished for an opportunity to rebuke him for it. When
             bidding good evening I introduced myself to the Gen-
             eral who very cordially shook me by the hand. I
             addressed him thus, "General, I am somewhat jealous
             of you. You never come to Mass or to hear me preach
             on Sunday, although you go to hear other chaplains.
             I have a most ardent desire for your conversion and
             would hope to effect it should you come to hear me."
             These remarks drew forth a roar of laughter from the
             company. The General somewhat embarrassed said,
             "Well, Father, I'll try to make amends. Let me know
             the next time you have service and I will go to hear
             you."

Sept. 1   Leave camp for Orange Court House for the purpose
             of seeing General Ewell and find him in his quarters.
             The General seemed to be in a bad humor with the
             Protestant Chaplains of his corps. Having received me
             in his usually kind manner he asked me if I heard of
             the Council of Protestant Chaplains held at Orange
             Court House the other day. I answered, "No." "Well,"
             said he, "what do you think if they did not hold a
             council and decide it to be a mortal sin to go to a party.
             What do you think of that, Father?" I told him it was
             no sin in itself, but it might be very sinful under some
             circumstances. The truth is that for some weeks previous
             there was nothing but parties and officers riding about
             with young ladies, whilst our poor men were confined
             to the camp and living on short rations.

             So I was glad he introduced the subject in order to
             give me an occasion of expressing my opinions. "But,

* Major General Edward Johnson, C.S.A. He was now commander of one of the three
divisions of Ewell's Second Corps.

General, you must not misunderstand me. I say to go to a party is not in itself a sin. However, parties now are entirely out of place and have a very demoralizing effect upon your men. How do you think our soldiers must feel, confined in their camp, and living on such rations as they now get whilst they see their officers riding about the country, gallanting ladies, indulging in luxuries and at the same time neglecting their business? I tell you, General, these parties had better be stopped or they will do much injury to your men. It is not the time for them."

Sept. 5

At Orange Court House

Major Kelly* has an altar built and some Protestant ladies spend the afternoon in decorating it. A strange sight to see an altar in a Methodist church!

Sunday, Sept. 6

Same place

I heard some confessions this morning and had Mass at 11. I had a very large congregation so much so that I feared the galleries might break down. I observed a good many Protestant officers and some citizens present. The Protestant portion of my audience with the exception of two persons behaved very well. These two, I think, will know better how to behave themselves the next time they attend Catholic service. That is if they remember the advice I that day gave them at the conclusion of my sermon. I was very much pleased at the large attendance of our Catholics. Owing to the late hour of the Mass, the heat of the weather, and the length of the sermon I was pretty well exhausted.

In the afternoon I visited Major Kelly and spent a short time at his quarters. From there I repaired to the Headquarters of General Ewell. The General was not

* Probably Major James Rigney Kelly, born in Ireland.

present but Doctor McGuire,* Colonel Pendleton** and several other members of the staff invited me to a seat. The General's quarters are in front of a splendid mansion situated about ½ mile from Orange Court House and on the summit of a high hill from which you have a vision of the surrounding country.

I was introduced by the Adjutant General to the strangers present, at least to those who had been strangers to me. The whole company expressed their sorrow that I should not preach that afternoon as they were intending to go and hear me. I remarked that fasting till 1 p.m., celebrating Mass, and preaching a long sermon were labor enough for one day. But added that I should be willing to preach for them any day it would contribute to their profit as well as their pleasure. One of the staff, a large corpulent man said to me, "Father, do you think you could send me to heaven?" Looking at him I remarked, "Captain, I fear you have too much beef about. I think I would have hard work to bring you as far as Purgatory." The Captain now became the subject of a general laugh.

Sept. 12   Today I paid a visit to General Ewell. He received me as usual very kindly, complimented me for the bold manner in which I denounced the conduct of some of the officers of my brigade, told me to continue to do so, regardless of the consequences. I thanked him for his encouraging words and told him I would always do my duty as a Catholic priest.

That Father Sheeran's direct methods were effective is suggested by one of his diary entries:

* Dr. Hunter McGuire, medical director of the "Valley" Army.
** Lieutenant-Colonel Alexander S. Pendleton, now chief of Artillery of the Army of Northern Virginia.

Date and place unspecified, but apparently at about the same time and location as entry immediately preceding

Some of the Protestant officers of this battery expressed their gratitude on account of the effects of my last visit. They told me of two notorious drunkards who had not drunk a drop since they had seen me before and were now giving an edifying example to their companions whom they formerly scandalized by their bad conduct. These gentlemen not knowing better attributed to me personally what should be attributed to the graces of the sacraments.

He was having large crowds at his Masses; he was often hearing confessions until late at night; the numbers who received Holy Communion were consistently large. On one Sunday in September, as we have seen, he had at his Mass "a very large congregation, so much so that I feared the galleries might break down." This reference to "galleries" recalls another interesting feature of his apostolate. That morning he was again celebrating Mass in the Orange Court House Methodist Church, gladly offered to him for that purpose by the Protestants. The Protestant ladies, he reports, again spent the previous afternoon in decorating his altar, specially built for the occasion by an army officer. Many Protestants were present at the Mass, as they were also at many of his services elsewhere. It was not unusual for a Protestant officer to give up his tent to be used as a confessional. On one occasion a Jewish ordnance sergeant insisted on doing the same.

He was always treated with the greatest cordiality by General Ewell. The following episode is typical:

Sunday, Sept. 12

When I was about to bid him goodbye [after a visit at the General's headquarters] the General chidingly remarked, "Father, you have never called to see Mrs. Ewell notwithstanding the many invitations sent you." "Well, General, I am not a great hand to visit, nor to mingle much in society unless my business calls me. But did I know when I should find Mrs. Ewell without company I would certainly do myself the pleasure of calling to see her." "Well, Father, you will find her without company today, and I know she will be very glad to see you as she often speaks of you." [A later

Sept. 12, afternoon entry in the diary reports:] Pay Mrs. Ewell a visit; kindly received by her; converse about my friends in Nashville with whom she was well acquainted and on various religious subjects. Bid her goodbye and return to camp.

His easy relations with Ewell admitted even reciprocal badinage:

Oct. 13

Lee is again moving northward against Meade

At 6 this morning we commenced our march in the direction of Warrenton and pass many abandoned camps. As yesterday I had the misfortune of losing my overcoat and as this morning was quite cold, I wrapped a grey blanket around me. Thus robed, sitting on my horse and from a hill viewing the surrounding scenery, General Lee and staff passed but I think did not recognize me. Soon after General Ewell and staff rode up, the General exclaiming, "Why, Father, were you in the battle yesterday?" "Why do you ask?" "I see you have a Yankee blanket and I thought you captured it." "I was at the battle, General, but I captured nothing. Some of *your good boys* stole my overcoat, so I have to wear my blanket." The whole company roared out laughing when they heard that the boys began to steal from me.

There were good reasons why his military chiefs respected their Catholic chaplain. His influence over the men enabled him, at least once, to quell an incipient riot that a general could not control:

Sept. 14

Shortly before the push north-

This morning at 1 we received marching orders. The camp is soon all commotion, men cooking rations, etc. We march at daylight, pass through Orange Court House, but know not our destination. We halt in a field

ward had some two miles east of Orange Court House. The sun
started is now excessively hot and there being no shade our
men are exposed to its burning rays for the greater part
of the day.

We were soon followed by those vultures of the army,
the sutlers, who with their wagons of merchandise took
up a position on the side of the road. On this day Gen.
Johnson being absent, the Brigadier General was in
command of our division. His overofficiousness in his
temporary command rendered him an object of hatred
and ridicule to some of our Brigades, and many of the
boys availed themselves of this occasion to manifest their
feeling.

Some of the boys were engaged in plundering the
sutlers' wagons of their precious contents. Now the
General in his anxiety to preserve discipline was with
his staff constantly riding along our lines, receiving
hisses and groans from unknown voices as he passed.
This irritated him much and he made many but unsuccessful efforts to find out the authors. At length one
of the 15th La. regiment became the object of his indignation. The fellow was detected in stealing a bottle
of wine from one of the sutlers, and for this offence the
General had him stand on a gate post for some two
hours, exposed to the view of the division. Seeing, however, that the efforts of the commander were unable to
protect the sutlers' wagons, I repaired to the scene of
plunder and sent the men to their commands.

He continued not to mince words in defending the principles for which
the South was fighting. Near Bristoe, as the army paused for a few
hours, he had a heated discussion with a Yankee prisoner:

Oct. 16   During our conversation several inquisitive and vulgar
specimens of Yankees drew near to hear what was going

on. One of them apparently anxious to show his smart-
ness and patriotism addressed me saying, "Don't you
fellows think we ain't going to enlist again when our
term expires!" I turned round and observed, "I was
not talking to you, sir." "You will be tarnation fooled
if you think any such thing," he replied, "for every
man of us will reenlist." One of his companions told
him he was a "darned sight mistaken for he was one
that would never fire a shot after his time expired."

In the meantime up comes a true-blooded Yankee
somewhat advanced in years but full of a sense of his
own knowledge and importance, and very anxious to
enlighten my mind on the military and political events
of the day. I told him I came not to discuss politics
but to see his Catholic fellow-prisoners. The fellow
wanted to "spout" and spout he would no matter what
I would say: "There are many traits in the Southern
character which I admire but their encroachments on
the rights of the North have been so long and frequent
we could no longer stand it. Yes, sir! we were willing
to divide with them the offices of the government, to
trade with them, and to treat them as our equals." "Is
that really so?" said I. "Our country, sir," continues
Mr. Yank, "is now more prosperous than before the
war, our debt is smaller and currency better than at
any time in our history. Our trade and commerce is
flourishing as it never did before, and we are daily
advancing in your territory. Yes, sir. We have now
Arkansas, Texas, Louisiana, Mississippi, Kansas, Tennessee and a large portion of Alabama and we will soon
have possession of the whole coast."

Here I interrupted the orator by remarking that they
were advancing the wrong way during the last few days
in Virginia. "That makes no difference, sir, it is but a

small affair. We are determined to fight for our flag and put down the rebellion, cost what it may, and we have men and money enough to do it." "You appear, sir, to be a man of no ordinary knowledge for really you know every thing. Will you be kind enough to let me know what great man I have the pleasure and honor of knowing?" "I am no great man, sir, but I am a man of years and experience." "That you have years to recommend you is evident, but that you have anything else I deny. It would be hard to tell which predominates in your character, ignorance or impudence. I told you I desired no controversy with you, but you give us an exhibition of your ignorance about Northern rights, Southern aggressions, Federal prowess, Yankee trade and commerce, and all such stuff as you find hashed up in your mercenary papers, and you have been impudent enough to make this exhibition of your ignorance for the purpose of enlightening a Catholic priest. Now, sir, I would not honor you with a controversy on these subjects nor would I notice you, but, lest you might construe my silence as an assent to your effusion of ignorance, [I say that] you, sir, might make a good speech when electioneering for the office of township constable, but your language and ideas disqualify you for any higher office." "Well," said he, "I am a prisoner and I must put up with this." "You get what you deserve, sir. I wished to spare your feelings, but you would not let me."

This ended my visit to the Yankee prisoners.

Nor was the chaplain's patience impregnable toward Southerners who acted disloyally. A few weeks previously had occurred this incident:

Sept. 19   The night was cold, and our staff wagons containing blankets and tents were not up, so we were in a rather unpleasant situation. Our horses, too, were suffering as they had nothing to eat all day and were after a long march. I sent my orderly to a farmer who had plenty of corn in order to get some feed for our horses. The farmer, although having plenty, positively refused to sell any. I sent the orderly back to offer the money, and if he would not take it, to take the corn and I would abide by the consequences. The horses had a good supper.

It would be unfair, however, to accuse Father Sheeran of a lack of the gentler attributes. He even had, at times, a rather mild and clerical sense of humor:

Oct. 13   Old Mrs. Semmes, the mother of the Senator,* and several other ladies of Warrenton were so rejoiced at the reported approach of our army that they remained up all night cooking and baking, and had prepared breakfast for a large number of our men. Indeed the good people of this place were almost beside themselves with delight. The ladies in particular, many of whom *kissed* Generals Lee and Ewell.

When about bidding the Semmes family goodbye Miss Clara begged of me to remain and she would go for her mother; she knew she wanted to see me. Soon the good old lady came, almost out of breath from the excitement. She too grasped me by the hand and made other demonstrations of affection. "O, Father," she said, "I had the pleasure of kissing the hand of General Lee this morning, and the good General Ewell whom I knew from his infancy." "Yes, Father," said Miss Clara, "and she kissed him too and embraced him." "Well, Mrs. Semmes, really if that is the case I will have to

---

* Thomas Jenkins Semmes, born in Georgetown, D. C., served in the Confederate Senate.

tell Mrs. Ewell." "Father, if you do, you must tell her that it was a lady of some eighty years that did so."

On October 24, 1863, he arrived at Richmond to begin his longest furlough of the war. One night shortly before leaving camp he was in a meditative mood:

Oct. 8   Soon our shelter tents were pitched, and the boys were seated by their comfortable fires and emptying or lightening their haversacks of some of the rations prepared before leaving camp. I know not if it is to be attributed to the state of my mind at the time but I thought this one of the most impressive scenes I had ever witnessed. The men now comfortably seated on one side of their fires, their brilliantly polished arms in stacks glistening on the other, the columns of light ascending from below and reflected by the boughs of the majestic oaks above, formed a strange combination of ideas, and in my opinion presented a beautiful subject for the pen of the poet or the pencil of the artist. The arches formed by the boughs above reminded me of the Gothic arches of some of our large cathedrals, but there is nothing else to complete the simile. Instead of the devout worshippers *there* adoring the God of peace and praying for the salvation of their enemies, *here* are men drilled in the science of war, many of them knowing little and caring less about their God, armed with deadly weapons and about to meet their fellow-men on the bloody field of battle. Hence I say these scenes presented to my mind a strange combination of ideas.

At Richmond Father Sheeran obtained permission to lengthen his furlough by taking a trip through the deep South, where he had many friends. He left the Confederate capital on November 3, and traveled by leisurely stages through North Carolina, Georgia, and Alabama.

He was delighted to find himself greeted at various places by former members of the Army of Northern Virginia. For example, at Mobile:

Nov. 25   This afternoon I met many old friends from the Army of Virginia. One was surprised that I did not at first recognize him. "Ah, Father, don't you remember when you attended to me in the ambulance coming off the battlefield of Williamsburg?" I then of course remembered him. The grateful feelings expressed by this poor fellow now with but one arm I shall never forget. "My heart jumped," said he, "when I saw you in the pulpit on Sunday. The Catholics of Mobile know you by hearing of what you have done for our boys in Virginia."

At Atlanta he had an even more pleasant reunion:

Dec. 3   As the Reverend Father O'Riley* informed me that no person was permitted to go to the front without a pass from headquarters, I telegraphed to Colonel Brent,** the Adjutant General of Bragg† to send me down a pass. Believing that General Lee's pass, which I had with me, would suffice as it did in all other places, I called at the Provost's office to inform him [that] if I did not soon get an answer to my telegram, I should start on General Lee's pass. He told me if I did I would find myself arrested.

Promenading round Atlanta this afternoon I saw a young man watching me very closely. I was not a little surprised when he called me by name. "Sir," said I, "you have the advantage of me. I do not know who

---

* Possibly Fr. Michael O'Reilly, listed in the *Catholic Directory* as being stationed at Frostburg, Va.

** This could be any one of the four following: Colonel Burr C. Brent, 2nd. Maryland State Guards; Lieutenant Colonel Charles B. Brent, 4th Battalion, Kentucky Cavalry; Colonel George W. Brent, of Beauregard's Staff; Colonel Preston Brent, 38th Mississippi Cavalry.

† Major General Braxton Bragg, C.S.A.

you are." "Father," said he, "do you not remember General H. Cobb's* courier on the Peninsula?" I soon recognized him as an old friend from Ship Point near Yorktown. He told me General Cobb was in town and would be very glad to see me.

I called at the General's headquarters and he gave me a warm reception. He inquired about the old 14th, said he had heard much of its bravery. We talked much of our marches and countermarches, reviews, Yankee hunts etc., old Bankhead McGruder** on the Peninsula. "Father," said he, "do you know what we used to say about the 14th when we were at Yorktown?" "I do not know that I do." "You know," said he, "how old Z. used to swear. Well the common saying was that the men of the 14th La. were the most favored in the service, for while they had Z. to damn them, they had Father Sheeran to save them." The General then asked me where I was bound for. I told him for Bragg's army and informed him also about the cause of my delay. He immediately telegraphed up to the front and the following day provided me with a pass.

On the steamboat (Nov. 15), carrying him from Montgomery to Selma he was repeatedly accosted by old soldiers of Lee's campaigns.

The only unpleasant incident of the whole journey occurred while Father Sheeran was traveling by train to Atlanta. Because of the light it throws on his character this encounter will be given in full, in his own words:

Dec. 2   As we approach Atlanta ladies carrying work to the city began to crowd into the cars. The most of them were young women or girls engaged in making clothes for the army; but according to the modern doctrine of

---

* This must be Brigadier General Thomas Reade Rootes Cobb, C.S.A. His brother was the Confederate senator, Howell Cobb. Father Sheeran may have confused the two names.
** Major General John Bankhead Magruder, C.S.A.

woman worship every gentleman, no matter how old or infirm, must relinquish his seat for every Madame or Miss or anything else wearing petticoats. This morning as I felt so unwell, and having a right to my seat, I resolved to disregard this custom of gallantry and hold on to my place. As the ladies came in, all the gentlemen, excepting myself, relinquished their positions for the sake of the more favored if not the gentler sex.

Soon these fair daughters of Georgia crowded in so rapidly as not only to occupy all the seats, but even to crowd up the aisle.

Now my position was anything but agreeable. I was the observed of all observers. 'Ladies' and gentlemen had their eyes constantly upon me. Had nature gifted me with anything of a handsome exterior I might misconstrue the cause of attraction, but I was satisfied I was not the object of admiration, but rather of scorn and contempt. However I mustered *brass* enough to bear it. My standing traveling companions did not long confine themselves to observations, but soon gave expression to their feelings.

A 'gentleman' would say in a rather elevated voice, 'It is customary for gentlemen to give up their seats to the ladies!' Again a Georgia Miss of perhaps some twelve or fourteen and with her mouth ornamented with tobacco juice would say, 'Look at that man sitting whilst ladies are standing!'

I resolved to practice patience and holy indifference; but a burly fellow standing alongside compelled me to break my resolution. Wishing no doubt to win the admiration of his *fair* traveling companions, and make me cognizant of the etiquette of this enlightened age, he addressed me in a loud voice and in sweet Scotch accent, saying, 'It is customary for gentlemen to give up their seats to ladies,' thus attracting not only my attention but that of the bystanders.

Looking at him for a moment I asked, in a manner to be well understood, 'Who sent you here to teach lessons in etiquette? If *you* are a gentleman you know that it is the place of a gentleman to mind his own business. When I wish to take lessons in politeness I will go to some person able to instruct me.' This rebuke caused Mr. —— [?] and others to turn their eyes and attention in some other direction. I held on to my seat 'like grim death to a nigger', notwithstanding the efforts made to remove me. But I must confess that this was *my* hardest battle of the war. My journey from Montgomery to Atlanta I shall ever remember. I was unwell when going aboard the cars, and the loss of rest and the scenes there exhibited were not calculated to improve my health, or even permit an equilibrium of the stomach.

Saints of God, anxious for the salvation of souls, pious theologians, and men of spiritual experience, knowing the power of concupiscence, and the weakness of our fallen nature, have universally cautioned men to avoid as much as possible the company of females. But had these masters of spiritual science ever made a railroad trip in a ladies' car in north Georgia, they would no doubt all agree that this would be an exceptional case.

For just imagine a company of females with complexions not of the pretty brunette, but rather resembling that of a sunburnt potato; imagine them including the wife of the wealthy planter, the woman of middling circumstances, and the peasants' [?] less graceful daughters, all with snuff boxes and small wooden spoons and filling their mouths with this disgusting pulverized weed; imagine then that when under the influence of this stimulating indulgence, they, when laughing, show their dirty snuff-colored teeth, exhibiting their lips covered with this disgusting looking stuff oozing out of their mouths; then take a glance on the floors below, now covered with their surplus tobacco fluid, and resembling somewhat a duck pond in the spring of the year; imagine next the dense sea of atmosphere with tobacco pent up in a close car; and tell me what would be the consequence of associating with such females? I will not pretend to answer for others; but, had I never seen women before these met with on my trip through North Georgia, I should look upon them as some of God's ugliest and most disgusting creatures. I wish I had not made a note on this subject, for it almost sickens me to think of the snuff-eaters of Georgia.

Reaching Dalton, Georgia, on December 7, he agreed, a few days later, to substitute briefly for the absent Catholic chaplain of Bragg's army, then encamped near the town. He was with the troops long enough (Dec. 15, 16) to prepare for baptism a soldier who for some offense was condemned to be shot. Next day on returning to the prison to administer this Sacrament, Father Sheeran found that the man — having balanced the spiritual and temporal opportunities — had escaped during the night.

While camping out near Dalton one night the chaplain had a chance to compare the outdoor sleeping conditions of Georgia and Virginia (Dec. 18): "Without a fire all night, with my light covering of blankets and storm-perforated tent I would certainly freeze; and with a fire and no one to watch [it] I would certainly be burned up. Fortunately some of the boys volunteered to take turns in guarding me and the fire during the night."

He began his return journey northward on December 21 and two days later preached in the church at Macon: "There were a large number of Protestants . . . among whom were all the young ladies of the Female Academy, led more by curiosity, no doubt, than by devotion, to hear the Confederate chaplain."

Next he visited a Georgia village called Fort Valley, which he describes in highly uncomplimentary terms:

> I went out to see the city of Fort Valley. I cannot well describe this place for it is indescribable. It contains about a dozen houses, some of which, it would appear, were built as *ventilators* for the surrounding country. They have doors on all sides, and as the people of Georgia never close their doors, one feels whilst sitting in one of those houses, as if the "Trade Winds" were concentrated on his precious person, a sensation not very agreeable in cold weather.

Here he picked up a fellow traveler:

Dec. 28
> Fort Valley appeared to me to be one of the last places in creation for a Catholic to locate himself. I was sorry to see Mr. Gleason* and his daughter here. I felt more for the daughter than for Mr. Gleason for, whilst he could spend his time hunting and fowling, she was doomed to a kind of solitary confinement, which was seldom interrupted save by a very infrequent visit from one of the lemon-faced snuffeaters of Georgia. I objected to Mr. Gleason retaining his daughter in such a position and suggested that he should send her to the Academy in Richmond where she might be improving her mind until circumstances permitted her return home. He yielded to my suggestion so I resolved to take her with me to Virginia.

This decision of Father Sheeran's is perhaps partly explained by a very important incident that had occurred in his life a little less than three years before. His own daughter, Isabella, who had taken her vows in 1858, had died in February, 1861, a few weeks before her eighteenth birthday. It is not surprising that his fatherly heart was touched by the plight of little Miss Gleason.

---

* Further details concerning this friend of Father Sheeran's are missing, including the gentleman's full name.

Father Sheeran was anxious to see Charleston, so he and his charge traveled up by way of Savannah to the South Carolina port. The city was at this time, of course, still under siege. The fact was illustrated to Father Sheeran while he was speaking with the Catholic bishop of Charleston* (Jan. 14): "The bishop gave me a cheerful welcome. He lamented the fact that he could not invite me to stay with him during my sojourn, as he was compelled to abandon his house on account of the proximity of the shells. Whilst conversing, a large shell burst about two hundred yards from the house." But this was nothing compared with what was to follow.

* Right Reverend [sic, in *Catholic Directory*] P. N. Lynch, D.D.

Jan. 17   Agreeable to previous arrangement I said my Mass this morning in St. Joseph's church at 7 o'clock. Just before the communion Father Filion* made his announcement, saying in broken English, "My brethren, the Reverend Gentleman you see now at the altar is a Redemptorist and the chaplain of General Lee's army. He will preach for you today at the last Mass and I know will tell you many good things. He has stood up on twenty battlefields and was not afraid. (I here could hardly keep from laughing, thinking to myself, What a big one! I never was on a battlefield yet that I was not afraid.) You must not then be afraid of the Yankee shells today but come and hear the good father and bring your neighbors."

Well, ten o'clock came and with it an immense concourse of people. Father Filion said a low Mass while the choir sang some beautiful pieces. The church was literally packed: pews, aisles and galleries. The sermon was on Mortal Sin, and was listened to with the most profound attention for about half an hour when suddenly the whole congregation as if by instinct set their ears and in a few seconds more comes a hundred pound Parrott shell whizzing directly over the roof of the church and ploughs right into the earth some fifty yards distant.

Suddenly I heard a wild yell in the organ loft, next

---

* Father Sheeran's spelling is incorrect. The priest was Father L. Fillion of Charleston.

71

something tumbled downstairs, and now some half dozen of people ran to the door and most of the congregation jumped to their feet. For a second I felt something of the panic of fright, but I soon overcame my feeling and addressed the congregation in an authoritative tone and commanded them to keep their places, asking, "What are you all afraid of? Do you think God is not able to protect you from Yankee shells? Is He not able to protect you in the church as well as out of it? Keep still, there is not one bit of danger." Before I gave them any time for reflection I resumed my sermon, and infused into it as much animation as possible. The good people seemed to forget all about the shells and not being disturbed by another they listened during another half hour with the most earnest attention. But no sooner were they dismissed than they crowded to the adjacent lot to get a view of the shell. I soon followed them and advised them to disperse and go home lest they receive another unwelcome visitor.

The travelers reached Richmond on January 25, 1864. Miss Gleason was consigned to the care of the Sisters at the "asylum," while Father Sheeran made some meditations on what he had observed during his Southern swing:

Jan. 21   In my travels through the South, although I had met
(date of   with much personal kindness, I found the stay-at-homes
this   having but one great object in view, that is, the making
entry)   of money. Never had I seen such avariciousness as that
                displayed throughout my travels, but more particularly
                in Georgia. Money and their negroes appeared to be
                their gods, and for these they were not only willing to
                sacrifice their own children, who were now fighting the
                battles of their country, but even the country itself.

All the more reason, then, for action by those who *were* loyal and energetic! And, as Father Sheeran soon learned, there was a new need:

Jan. 29   During my short sojourn [at Richmond] I received a message from Colonel York, who is now out with the command,* giving a gloomy picture of the condition of the regiment, and urging me by all means to come out as soon as possible. From other sources I learned that our men were very much dissatisfied on account of the way they had been treated during the winter and that some of them were even deserting. Knowing the kind of materials our boys were made of and the influence I was able to exercise over them, I resolved to go to camp immediately.

Father Sheeran caught up with his brigade at Orange Court House on February 5, 1864.

At this time the posture of military affairs in Virginia was as follows: the Army of the Potomac, still commanded by Meade, was poised just north of the Rapidan, with its headquarters at Culpeper Court House, about 25 miles northwest of Fredericksburg. Meade's strategic intention was simple: to mount an offensive against Richmond and end the war. It was Lee's aim to block him, or, at least, to slow him up and make him pay a heavy cost for his advances. In that first week of February, on the south side of the Rapidan, the Confederates faced Meade and waited grimly.

From this point on, Father Sheeran may speak for himself.

Letter dated Feb. 7, to his ward in Rich- mond**   [On one cold February night near Orange Court House he was invited by a medical corpsman to sleep in an ambulance for greater warmth.] I thanked him and accepted his kind offer; but what a night I spent! The night was cold and I was wet and without blankets. But this was not all. There were four horses tied to the wheels of the ambulance. For about an hour these poor animals made the most unharmonious noise mas- ticating the corn they so greedily devoured; and of course with the most comfortable bed I could not sleep.

* Colonel Zebulon York, of 14th Louisiana Infantry.
**See *supra*, p. xi, for Father Sheeran's utilization of this epistolary device.

Having disposed of their corn and no doubt feeling the good effects of it, they began the exercise of *rolling*. One would give the ambulance a jerk in one direction, another would soon counteract this by a sudden pull in another, and thus for nearly two hours they rock me not to sleep but out of all patience and frequently nearly out of the ambulance. . . .

Feb. 14

At Picket Post, Morton's Ford, on Rapidan

I am sorry to inform you that some five of those very men who helped to whip the enemy have now gone over to them, to seek no doubt better rations than our corn meal and salt beef. That they will ever return I doubt much. . . .

Feb. 17

On way back from Picket Post to main camp, "some seven miles from Orange C.H., on the Fredericksburg plank road"

For some time I rode along with the brigade, now marching at the gait of four miles an hour, but fearing even at that pace I should be frozen before reaching camp. I put spurs to my grey and made General Ewell's headquarters, a distance of nearly five miles, in about half an hour. Mrs. Ewell seeing me approach met me at the door with expressions of sympathy. My feet and hands were almost powerless, and were I to judge from the sense of feel I would conclude that I had not any face on my head.

The General invited me to the fire now burning very cheerfully, but Mrs. Ewell interposed and made use of other remedies before permitting me to get close to the heat. I shall ever remember her kindness to me this morning. Soon the blood began to circulate freely and I once more had the use of my tongue. I spent about an hour and a half before a good fire and in agreeable conversation.

Mrs. Ewell is a lady of more than ordinary intellectual powers, well educated and for one of her sex remarkably well posted on military and political matters. In religion she is a rigid Episcopalian, somewhat fond of discussing religious subjects, but very respectful when speaking of Catholic dogmas. During the early part of our conversation today she asked me several moral questions and appeared much pleased that my answers were according to her previously expressed opinions.

One of her questions was, "Father, do you think a general is justified in carelessly exposing himself on the battlefield?" "No mam! I think he is not. A general is the soul of the army, and his fall always causes despondency and sometimes greater disaster to his command. A general in my opinion should keep himself as far as possible out of danger, but in such a position as to see or hear of the movements in battle, but there may arise circumstances which would require even a general to expose himself to every danger." "There now, General," said she, looking at her husband, "you see that the Father is just of my opinion." From this remark I concluded that she and the General had been discussing the subject.

At this stage of the conversation our brigade was just passing, so after refusing a pressing invitation to stay for dinner I mounted my horse and started with our boys for camp.

Feb. 18

Still in same camp

Last night was one of the coldest of the winter. My bed was uncomfortably hard and covering very scanty, hence I slept very little. I paid a visit to the guard house this morning and heard serious complaints from some of the poor fellows there confined. One of them showed his rations for the day and on weighing it I found it was short one-fourth of the regular allowance. Having heard many complaints before with regard to short rations I determined this morning to investigate the matter and find out who were cheating the men.

I first called upon the commissary of the 10th La. Reg., who had issued the short rations which I had carried with me, asking the amount he had drawn for each man. He answered ¼ lb. corn meal etc. "Here, sir, is a ration you issued this morning. Weigh it." He did so and found it deficient. "Now, sir, there has been too much of this work going on. Poor men are cheated out of their already scanty rations, hence so many complaints, murmurs and even desertions. This work must be stopped. I shall report the matter to General Johnson." The fellow begged off, saying it was a mistake, and if I would make no complaint he would see that the like would not happen again. We had fewer complaints about rations afterwards.

Feb. 24

In camp

Father Smulders reached here yesterday looking indeed not very well. Today I brought him round the different regiments in order to make him acquainted. I had the Catholics assembled in their respective quarters and I delivered to them a brief address exhorting them to prepare for their Easter communion now while we were enjoying a brief repose. I was much pleased to see them so well disposed. You would, I know, be delighted were you here last Sunday to see the large congregation I had at Mass. They were from all the surrounding commands. After Mass I announced that I would preach a sermon at 3 p.m. and invited not only Catholics but also Protestants. The weather has been beautiful and at the appointed hour a great number were assembled, but seeing many were yet coming I did not begin till 3½.

I was truly delighted with the strict attention and

good conduct of the Protestant portion of my audience. I trust in God some favorable impressions have been made. That same evening one of the Protestant officers expressed his intention of becoming a Catholic and others requested that I should preach every Sunday afternoon. Some few of the green Virginians were heard to say, "I wonder where that father gets such pretty things," meaning my alb and stole. I am pleased to inform you that the spirit of our men is much improved, and the great majority of our brigade have reenlisted for the war.

When I came to camp Colonel York was commanding, and of course I messed at brigade headquarters, but he, being relieved by a senior Colonel returned to the regiment. The boys went immediately and built me a house which, I know, you would be delighted to see. There is a very handsome brick chimney, a nicely furnished mantelpiece and a well-laid floor. This morning Father Smulders and I said Mass in my new mansion and he is now occupied in hearing confessions. Next Monday Father Smulders will start for Charleston and I will commence my grand rounds of the army of the Potomac or of North Virginia. Pray, my child,* that my mission may be successful and that I may have time to visit all our Catholic soldiers before we commence active service.

My health is remarkably good, but I am sorry to say my eyes yet give me some anxiety. I hope God will give me the privilege of *seeing* my way home after this cruel war is over. However, I will endeavor to prepare myself for a contrary privation.

---

* The reference is, of course, to his ward in Richmond.

Sunday,   The weather is most delightful this morning re-
Feb. 28   minding us that Spring is at hand. The gentle rays of
           the morning sun, the soft and balmy Southern breeze,
In camp   the solemn stillness of the camp, and the cheerful coun-
           tenances of so many of our men who received com-
           munion this morning, make impressions on my soul
           which it would be vain to attempt to describe. In my
           checkered life, made up of so much of cares and
           anxieties, God has been kind enough to afford me some
           happy moments, but never have I felt more happy than
           whilst I write to you this morning.

           Whilst absent from camp I found on my return that
           the enemy of peace and charity has been making his
           ravages among my men. The spirit of discord and in-
           subordination became so great as to cause several of our
           men to desert and even threatened to break up the
           organization of our brigade. This spirit the men tried
           to conceal from me but I soon discovered it. To check
           this evil I knew nothing was competent save the graces
           of the sacraments. I sent for Father Smulders and made
           known to him the state of affairs. After a consultation
           we resolved to make war on the enemy. . . . For the
           last four days we have been laboring at our respective
           posts and God has been kind enough to bless our efforts
           in a most remarkable manner; hence our camp this
           morning presents more the appearance of a religious
           community than an assemblage of rough soldiers.

During the next three weeks he makes his previously referred to
"grand rounds of the army of . . . North Virginia." He then returns to
the camp, from where he makes the following notations:

March 23   This morning the snow is 18 inches deep. I feel very
            much stiffened after my cold ride last evening. This was
            an exciting day about camp. Two of our divisions,

Johnson's and Rodes',* fought a regular scientific battle with snow balls. This was the first battle I had ever witnessed with pleasure. There were some 8,000 men engaged and the lines were so regularly formed, the movements so systematic, the officers displaying so much activity at the head of their commands, their men fighting so stubbornly, now advancing on their opposing column, now giving way before superior numbers that one would forget for a moment that it was merely a sham. At one time we would see a body of troops marching through an adjacent woods endeavoring to flank their enemy; soon a counter movement would be made. Now a charge and a yell and many prisoners captured. For nearly two hours this battle of snow balls lasted. Now commences a most amusing scene. Johnson's whole division commences a rapid retreat but with solid and unbroken lines. Rodes' division following them in the utmost disorder and almost exhausted with laughter. Now the order is given, "Halt! Change front! Charge!" Now commences one of the most amusing and laughable scenes. Rodes' division is routed and driven for over half a mile and even through their own camp. Our boys came home as proud as if they had gained a victory over the Yankees.

Several Protestant officers waited on me and requested that I should have "service" at the Court House on Sunday. I told them that I came for that purpose and would be very happy to have them and their friends present.

March 24   Having finished hearing [confessions] for the night I took a walk, as is my custom, to see and hear what was going on. Judge you, my child, what was my agreeable

---

* Major General Robert Emmett Rodes, C.S.A.

surprise when instead of the profanity I usually hear in a strange camp I heard the sturdy voices of many of our Catholic soldiers united in reciting the rosary of our dear Lady in an adjacent tent. I cannot describe to you the effect this event produced on my mind.

This night I took my supper on genuine coffee and *cannon balls,* made out of flour by Father Smulders' orderly. I thought to myself, whilst enjoying these luxuries, that God sends meat but the devil sends cooks.

On Sunday morning I heard some confessions and celebrated Mass at 8 a.m. This morning I had the consolation of giving First Communion to *three children,* ranging in age from twenty-five to forty.

Whilst sitting on my horse waiting for inspection to be over I could not refrain from viewing with singular emotions the scenes around me. To my right about 400 yards is Summerville Ford, the very spot where I first met Stonewall Jackson when on our way to the battle of Cedar Run. Some four miles to the North on that side of the Rapidan is Cedar Mountain from which our batteries dealt such destruction among the enemy at the battle of Cedar Run. I could see the spot on which the Louisiana Guards Battery fought its first battle and so nobly distinguished itself. On the opposite side of the river is a tree under which I had a long conversation with General Ewell on the way to the second battle of Manassas.

The captain furnished me with a courier who "knew every acre of land in this section of the country." He is indeed a singular specimen of the *genus homo.* He was born in Ireland — you would think he left there yesterday — had lived in Georgia for many years, owns thirty thousand acres of land in that state, has lost

First page of Father Sheeran's "Noviceship Autobiography."

home. She welcomes the Belgians, and the German Catholics. If she is wise, she will never welcome Yankees there, nor admit them, for they will be sure to play her some mean trick if she has anything to do with them.

The Monroe Doctrine is dead! It was never even mentioned in the Chicago, McClellan, Convention. Lincoln kicked over the clap-trap allusion to it, by the Baltimore Convention. The United States are not what they were. "*Peace* and amity" with all neighboring populations, is our wise course now. If Lincoln's Administration is wise it will recognize the Mexican Empire right away. We will sustain it in so doing. But, in tru h, we doubt very much wh ther the Emperor Maximilian cares the snap of his fingers whether Lincoln and Seward "recognize" him, or not. He will care a great deal more for a shipload of honest, unrevolutionary, Catholics, of various trades and occupations, who may be flying from these States. Mexico will take care of herself.

A GREAT AND CRUEL WRONG.

ARREST AND IMPRISONMENT OF A CONFEDERATE CATHOLIC CHAPLAIN.

The Rev. James Sheeran, of the congregation of the Redemptorists, formerly a priest of St. Alphonsus' Church in New Orleans, but, since 1861, a chaplain in the Confederate Army, is now a prisoner in Fort McHenry near Baltimore. We have known Father Sheeran for many years. We knew him while he was a layman, in Monroe, Michigan He is not only a devoted and excellent man, but one in the correctness of whose statements of fact the utmost reliance can be placed. Two or three weeks ago we received from him a short note of friendship, based on our old-time acquaintance. It informed us that he was within the Federal lines, at the Hospital at Winchester, Va., where, he told us, he was diligently engaged in affording spiritual consolations, and administering the Sacraments, to the sick and wounded of *both* the Confederate and Federal Armies.

On the day we are preparing this number of the *Freeman* for the press, we have been shocked and grieved at learning that Father Sheeran, notwithstanding his having a ' pass" from Gen. Wright, had been arrested, treated with gross indignity, thrown into a filthy guard-room among Federal soldiers who were confined there for drunkenness and bad conduct, and that, in this filthy prison, he was kept *five days*, obliged to listen to all the obscenity and blasphemies of the abandoned characters around him. The following letter, written by him to us from that prison, tells in simple language, and with an indignation natural to one of his hot and gallant Irish blood, the occasion and manner of his imprisonment.

MILITARY PRISON, Winchester, Va.

MY DEAR MR. McMASTER.—The correspondents of the public press have given glowing, if not very accurate accounts of General Sheridan's victories in the Valley. They have detailed minutely the number of rebels killed or prisoners taken, and of artillery captured. They have heralded to the world, even without a blush of shame for disgraced humanity, the number of barns, and of wheat and hay stacks burned, of houses plundered, of families impoverished and left without shelter or food—but there in one brave and chivalrous act which I believe no correspondent has yet noticed. On the 25th of Sept., or Ge-

I am pleased to say that I have received the kindest treatment from the officers and surgeons of Winchester, if I except Capt. ——, Adjt.-Gen. of Col. Edwards. I had occasion to call upon him, in company with another Catholic Priest, and I am sorry to say that the Captain acted in a manner both impertinent and ungentlemanly.

Last Saturday, hearing you were in town, I called at your quarters in order to make known to you my situation here. I was told, in a very rough manner, that I could not see you. Yesterday morning I called at your quarters for the same purpose, when, instead of an interview, a guard was sent for, and I was cast into a dirty prison, in company with drunken and blackguard soldiers, where I now remain.

I make these statements to you, General, not that I ask to be relieved, but that you may understand the state of the case. But I cannot help protesting against my treatment as a violation of good faith and a disregard of the protection given by a Federal general. Should I be retained in prison it will satisfy me that you, General, endorse the conduct of the post commander, and I am satisfied to let the public decide upon the merits of the case.

With much regard for your personal welfare, I remain, General, your humble servant,   JAMES SHEERAN.
Chaplain 14th La.

Nor has this been all. Father Sheeran, on the 8th instant, was transferred from Winchester to Baltimore, to be incarcerated in Fort McHenry. There, notwithstanding his distinct statement of his being a Catholic Priest, a man of *peace*, not of *war* ; a man of *mercy*, not of blood ; he was thrust into a "Slave-pen" and kept there two days and nights, among the most degraded of soldiers there imprisoned for various crimes. Father Sheeran remonstrated, in vain, that he was a *priest*, and that he had with him the consecrated oils, and other holy things of the Catholic religion, which ought not to be thus treated. All was in vain.

Thus far Father Sheeran's letters to us, from Winchester, Martinsbargh, and Baltimore.

We learn, now, also, that he is incarcerated in Fort McHenry. That he is denied the privacy that his sacred character should exact from any civilized power. That he is subjected to the ribaldry of disgraced Federal soldiers, imprisoned there for their crimes. That he has asked to have a visit from some Catholic priest, and been answered that he could see *no one*, as a visitor ; "You can see no one, nor can any one come to see you," were the words !

Now, t ll otherwise convinced, we must believe that there has, in this thing, been a *conspiracy* against Father Sheeran ; and that Gen. Sheridan is not acquainted with the facts. Gen. Sheridan has the reputation of an able and gallant soldier. He has, in some prints, been paraded in a vulgar list of Federal Generals, discriminated, very unwisely and improperly, as "Catholic Generals !" Gen. Sheridan's name, and his native, Perry county, Ohio, point him as a Catholic in religion, and, almost certainly, as a student under the good Dominican Fathers. If he be an instructed Catholic, he knows, well enough, that no priest can absolve him till he makes reparation for the outrage he has committed on Father Sheeran. The devil would clap his hands, and rejoice, at any absolution given him, without his entertaining the firm purpose of such reparation to the best of his power.

For, even if, as we charitably suppose, General Sheridan has been beguiled by some slippery member of his staff, now, so soon as he hears what has

Pages from *The Freeman Journal* ca... ing Father Sheeran's letters, wit... Mr. McMa... comments... the situatic...

neral Sheridan's army was advancing in line of battle on Harrisonburg, I resolved to enter his lines, and ask for a pass to Winchester, in order to attend to our wounded here. I was brought by a guard to General Wright, who commanded the advance. The General treated me very kindly, and commanded his Adjutant to give me a pass through the lines. I next met General Sheridan and staff, and introduced myself to his Adjutant, asking him for a pass to Winchester. He replied, "General Wright's pass is sufficient."

I called at all the hospitals from Harrisonburg to Winchester, and administered the Sacraments to some wounded soldiers. I reached Winchester, September 26th, since which time to October 31st, I have been daily ministering to the spiritual wants of the wounded of both armies, and doing what I could to aid them in other respects. Being desirous to see Gen. Sheridan on some business, and hearing he was in town, I called at the headquarters of Col. Edwards, commanding post at Winchester, where Gen. Sheridan was staying. To my great surprise, I was not only denied an admittance or audience, but was, by the order of Gen. Sheridan, cast into a dirty prison, the officer who executed his order, saying I was a "d—d old Catholic priest." From my prison I sent the General the following hastily written letter, and as I have as yet received no answer, I am forced to conclude that he endorses the conduct of his subordinate officers.

Let it be known, then, to the Catholics of the United States, that Gen. Sheridan has gained another victory, not over the defenceless women and children of the valley, but by throwing a Catholic priest into a dirty prison, to be the companion of drunken and disorderly soldiers, and this, too, when some of his own Catholic soldiers are dying without the sacraments.

JAMES SHEERAN,
Chaplain 14th La. Regt., C. S. A.

MILITARY PRISON, Winchester, Va., Nov. 1, 1864.

MAJOR-GEN. SHERIDAN.—DEAR SIR:—Fearing that you are not aware of the fact that a Catholic Priest has been cast into prison, on, or by command of Col. Elwards, I deem it my duty to make the following statement:

I am a Chaplain in the C. S. A. for the last three years and three months, and have been with he army of North ern Virginia, from the evacuation of Yorktown to the present time. On all the bloody fields of Virginia, Mary land and Pennsylvania, thousands of Catholic soldiers, of both armies, have received the Sacraments of the Church at my hands. Even at the late battle of Kernstown, the lamented Col. Mulligan, and many of his Catholic soldiers, were attended by me at their last moments.

Being absent from my command at the late battles of Winchester, and knowing that many Catholics might die without the Sacraments, I resolved to ask your permission to come and see after the wounded here. I entered your lines near Harrisonburg, and was brought to Gen. Wright, who, being satisfied I was what I professed to be, treated me very kindly, and gave me the enclosed pass. I met you and staff advancing through the fields on the right of the road, and told your Adjt.-Gen. my business, and asked a pass also of him. He replied that Gen. Wright's pass was sufficient. I continued my journey, and reached Winchester on the 26th of Sept., since which time I have ministered to the spiritual wants of all who called for me, and have attended the sick of your army, as well as of our own.

I am pleased to say that I have received the kindest treatment from the officers and surgeons of Winchester, if I except Capt. ——, Adjt.-Gen. of Col. Elwards. I had occasion to call upon him, in company with another Catholic Priest, and I am sorry to say that the Captain acted in a manner both impertinent and ungentlemanly.

Last Saturday, hearing you were in town, I called at your quarters in order to make known to you my situation here. I was told, in a very rough manner, that I could not see you. Yesterday morning I called at your quarters for the same purpose, when, instead of an inter-view, a guard was sent for, and I was sent into a dirty prison, in company with drunken and blackguard sol-

---

been done, be is bound to displace, and to court-martial, the Aid that has deceived him.

The imprisonment of Father Sheeran is an out-rage on the laws of war, for, as a non-combatant, as a minister of mercy to all, he held Gen. Wright's pass, which Gen. Sheridan's Chief of Staff pro-nounced "sufficient."

It was an outrage on religion. To solace and to comfort the wounded and the dying, Gen. Sheri-dan knows, is the work of a Catholic chaplain, without bothering as to which side they had been fighting on. The Priest of God, thus outraged while about "his Master's work," is defended by the ready vengeance of a jealous God! Nolite tangere christos meos! "Touch ye not my Anoint-ed, and do my Prophets no harm!"

It was an outrage on common decency. Father Sheeran has been in nearly all the great battles that have been fought in Virginia, in the last three years. His office of mercy has not been strained It has fallen, with equal charity, on Federals as on Confederates. Where bullets have whistled, and shells shrieked, and men were falling there, in a hundred battles, the devoted Redemptorist chap-lain gladly perilled his life, to speak hope, and faith, and love of God, to the dying — on either side, and, if instructed as Catholics, to give them the last Sacraments of the Church! The remnants of the Irish Brigade have reason to remember the little Irish Confederate priest, who lavished on them his spiritual, and also his tempo-ral aid, after Hooker's battle of Chancellorville, when, except for Father Sheeran, some of them would have died without the Sacraments. Father Sheeran, it was, that gave the last Sacraments to the gallant Col. Mulligan. If Gen. Sheridan hopes, as no doubt he does, to die as chivalrously as Mul-igan did, and as peacefully, let him hasten to make reparation to God and man for the outrage we have given thus much publicity to, in order that it may be remedied. In his latest note to us, from Fort McHenry, Father Sheeran writes:

"Is not this a beautiful recompense for one who devoted much of his time in binding up the wounds of unfortunate men left by Gen. Grant in his bloody march from the Ra-pidan to the James, during the month of May? Let the remnant of the Irish brigade know how the Catholic priest is treated, who cared for them on the battlefield of Chancellorsville, when Gen. Hooker abandoned them! Thank God, I labored not for the thanks or gratitude of men. My present treatment I will take as coming by the permission of God for some wise end, and will endeavo to bear it with patience. My great privation here is, that I have no opportunity of offering the Holy Sacrifice."

THE WAR!—ITS PROGRESS

Grant's army are building log-huts, &c., and going into winter quarters. So they say, and so it had best be. Grant has butchered and wasted some hundred and twenty thousand lives of his command, and has failed to take Richmond, the objective reason for those horrid hecatombs of hu-man sacrifices.

Sheridan has been hugging, more and more close-ly, the banks of the Potomac, at the very heel of the Shenandoah Valley, which he has been striving to lay waste. If the Confederates do not hold that

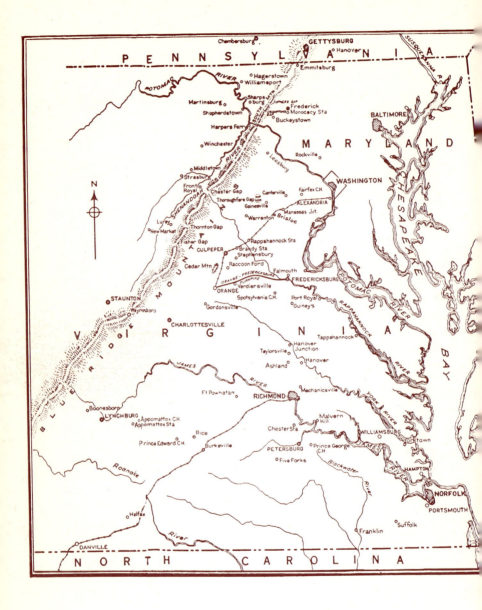

The area of Father Sheeran's military experiences.

some thirty thousand dollars by the war, complains much of the late currency act, has money and does not know what to do with it, has no wife but said he would like to get married. I soon discovered that he was an old tight-purse that no doubt starves himself to death for the sake of saving a little. I told him that the very best use he could put his money to was to give it to the orphans. They would pray for his soul and their prayers would be of much more value to him than money. The old fellow did not believe a word I told him.

Putting implicit confidence in him as a guide I paid no attention to where he was bringing me until he had me on the very bank of the Rapidan and in presence of the Yankee pickets. I asked him if ever the pickets shot across. He replied that they shot at him but had not hurt him. The day was now becoming extremely cold. Nevertheless the old fellow would talk and bother me about his money and land, about his friends at home, and about his college days — the fellow never went to a school higher than "Paddy Burn." I was thankful when I reached the camp of Posey's brigade as I expected to get rid of my travelling companion.

April 8   Although sick I celebrated Mass and had a very large congregation. During the forenoon, whilst lying on my camp cot, I received a letter from Captain Posey,* son of General Posey who was mortally wounded at the battle of Bristow last October. This young officer who is a convert but a most pious and exemplary Catholic, made a most pitiful appeal to me to come soon to see the Catholics of his brigade, for he did not know what day they might break up winter quarters. Having read

* Captain Ben Lane Posey, attached to 1st Regiment, Alabama Infantry, and, later, to 38th Alabama Infantry. His father was Brigadier General Carnot Posey.

this letter and concluding that it was of much more importance to take care of the souls of these brave men than to mind my own body, I immediately ordered my horse, packed up my vestments, blankets and other things and started for the Mississippi brigade now camped on the Rapidan near Clarks Mountain. Reaching there about 3 p.m. and feeling unwell I made an early bed time.

April 9

At camp near Clarks Mountain, Rapidan

It rains all day. Hear confessions all afternoon, although much indisposed. The rain pours down during the afternoon and night. Have a visit from General Harris* who welcomes me to his command, says he is not a Catholic himself but has much respect for the Catholic religion.

Sunday, . April 10

At same camp

The country is overflowed with water this morning so that we hardly could get a spot on which to pitch a tent for Mass. However about 8 a.m. having made such arrangement as we could, I offered up the Holy Sacrifice. There were many communions, but not wishing to keep the men standing too long in the mud and as it commenced to rain again I gave but a brief instruction. I yet felt very unwell but resolved to continue my mission. Having partaken of some refreshment I started at 10 a.m. for the camp of the 16th Mississippi.

April 12

Mass at 6½. Distributed communion to many, recited the rosary and preached a short sermon [at the Mississippians' camp]. After Mass I left for Orange Court House and reached there just in time to take the cars for Frederick Hall which I came to about 3 p.m. having travelled some fifty miles.

* General Nathaniel H. Harris, C.S.A.

Seldom have I met with such a reception as that given me this day by those patriotic sons of Maryland. Their countenances beamed with delight as I approached their quarters. Their camp was one of the best regulated and managed of any I had yet visited. Their log huts were neatly built and everything about them kept remarkably clean. Soon after my arrival a dinner was prepared which for cleanliness and variety would do honor to any of our hotels.

After dinner I told the boys I would remain with them but till the next morning as I had several other commands to visit, and did not know what time the whole army would be in motion. But I would hear all their confessions should it keep me all night. They did not keep me long idle and till 10 o'clock I had no rest. It was a laborious but most consoling night's work. I went to bed with my physical powers much exhausted.

April 13
At Frederick Hall camp

I heard confessions from about 5 till 7½ when I commenced Mass. This morning I shall never forget. During Mass I took sick and suffered everything but the agonies of death. I succeeded in finishing and gave communion to *everyone* present. Informing the men of the state of my health and requesting them to make a thanksgiving for the great grace they had just received I retired to an adjacent wood and took a rest upon a log praying that God would give the consecrated species time to decompose before I should be subject to further inconvenience. I soon recovered so far as to be able to take a cup of coffee and some other refreshment. Finding it impossible to continue my missions in my present state of health I resolved to retire to Richmond and rest for a few days.

April 19

At nearby camp of Wilcox's Alabama brigade

Having heard some confessions I said Mass at 7½. Announced that I should preach at 3½ and invited all to attend. This was quite a holiday in camp as the commanders relieved all those who wished to go to the "preaching" from all camp duties this day. The consequence was that at the appointed time I had an immense congregation. From a platform erected in the open air I addressed the assembled thousands for over an hour, and never was I more edified with the attention and good conduct of any audience. Although the day was somewhat cold every head was uncovered during the sermon. I spent about 1½ hours in the camp of the 1st Confederate Battalion hearing confessions and return at dark to the 8th Alabama.

April 21

Back at the main camp "on the Fredericksburg plank road"

I paid a visit to General Ewell who, always very kind, detailed a man to accompany me during the campaign and gave him a pass written by himself. He also gave me the privilege of taking with me a small tent. The General on this occasion asked me if I would not have "service" at his headquarters every other Sunday. I told him that there were too many Catholics who needed my services, but I might preach for them occasionally.

Sunday, April 24

At same main camp

Mass at 7½. We had an unusually large congregation as many came from other commands. A short instruction. Announced a sermon for 3½. At the appointed time an immense audience had assembled from the surrounding camp. Subject of the sermon was "Delay of Repentance." There was a large number of Protestants present who listened with respectful attention.

April 26

At same main camp

I believe I informed you that I had at length visited all the commands of the army excepting one brigade — Battle's* — now on picket. These I hope to visit tomor-

---

* Major General Cullen Andrews Battle, C.S.A.

row if we do not march. You can form no idea of the
consolation it affords me to think that all our good
Catholic soldiers have had an opportunity of making
peace with their God before meeting the enemy again
on the battlefields. This thought relieves my mind of a
great deal of anxiety, and I doubt not will have a tend-
ency to improve my bodily health, for it is perhaps my
misfortune that a naturally impetuous mind gives the
body no rest as long as important duties are unper-
formed. However this may be I find my health much
improved and am in very good spirits. But yet I cannot
banish from my mind the terrible prospect of the approaching conflict of arms.

What terrible subjects for meditation! Some two hundred thousand men, drilled in the art of murder anxious
to imbrue their hands in one another's blood, separated
only by a small stream, the waters of which are rapidly
falling and [our army is] hourly expecting orders to
march to the deadly combat. Would to God that I had
not to witness the approaching scenes of blood and
carnage! But I fear not the result for our cause. For if
a well disciplined army, approximating somewhat to the
enemy in numbers, well clad and well fed, and with
hearts glowing with the purest of patriotism and minds
determined to conquer or to die, are presages of victory
then we have much reason to hope. But in addition to
this I have an abiding confidence in the justness of our
cause.

May 4   Our infantry picketed the Rapidan from Morton's
Main   Ford on our extreme right to Liberty Bridge on our left,
camp   a distance of some 16 miles. Our camps did not extend
so far but were some 3 miles from and parallel with the
Rapidan. During the winter Ewell's corps occupied the
right and A. P. Hill's the left. Longstreet had but lately

returned from his East Tennessee campaign and with his now small corps was camped between Charlottesville and Gordonsville, or in the rear of A. P. Hill. The strength of our infantry at this time I know to be about as follows: Ewell's corps 15,000 muskets, A. P. Hill's 21,000 and Longstreet's, which consisted of two divisions, only about 11,000. We had a large proportion of artillery but the strength of our cavalry I do not know. The strength of the enemy, according to their own statements, amounted to over 200,000.

May 5   Up this morning at 4½; fed our horses, partook of a good breakfast, and were on the way at 5. At 8 a.m. we camp up with our brigade now drawn up in line of battle on the right of the Plank Road, running from Culpeper to Fredericksburg. I never saw our men more cheerful than on this occasion. The poor fellows had little idea of the terrible contest in which they were about to engage. [The Battle of the Wilderness is about to begin.]

We spent about two hours in this position when orders were given to advance. As we proceeded down the road through the Wilderness to near the place where "Stonewall" first attacked the Yankees at Chancellorsville, word came along the line that the enemy were in sight. Here our ambulances and medical wagons halted whilst our infantry moved forward and filed off to the left of the Plank Road.

Soon our sharpshooters were engaged in pretty lively exercise with the enemy now massed in the woods. Whilst several surgeons and myself were standing on the road watching the movements of our troops a solid shot from one of the enemy's guns came whizzing up the road and fell on a line parallel with us but about

50 yards off to the right. Being admonished by this un-expected and unwelcome visitor that our position was not very secure we fell back about a quarter of a mile where we resolved to establish our hospital.

In about an hour the terrible contest, known as the "Second Battle of the Wilderness" commenced. Ewell's whole corps is now engaged but owing to the dense wood is unable to keep a connected line. The battle which for the most part is a musketry one is terrific. Our thin and scattered lines deal destruction on the solid advancing columns of the enemy. The loss of human life is shocking. The ground is liberally covered with the dead and wounded of the enemy. Their lines waver, our boys press forward sending many prisoners to the rear. At length both lines come to a stand and for a moment appeared to be preparing for a more desperate effort.

Here occurred some little circumstances, which al-though trifling in themselves, will give us some insight to the character of our men and their cheerfulness in time of battle. Colonel York, who had just discontinued the pursuit of the Yankees, now charges after a fox running along our lines. Suddenly a wild turkey starts out from the undergrowth and our boys letting out a wild yell pour a volley after the affrighted bird. Soon a rabbit jumps out in front and makes in the direction of the enemy. Some of the boys pursue and bring back the animal amidst the cheers of their companions. These recreating scenes lasted but for a short time.

The work of human slaughter recommenced.

May 7   This was one of my most laborious days: it being spent from morning till late at night in hearing con-fessions, administering Extreme Unction, baptizing, and in washing and dressing wounds. Late this night we received orders to prepare to march in the morning. I threw myself down for a few hours in the open air but slept little.

May 16

At a hospital near Spotsylvania Court House

An amusing little occurrence took place this morning. Two of our regiment having strayed into the enemy's lines came up to two Yankees with muskets. The Louisianians were without arms but not without tongues. Finding there was no time for ceremonies one of them yelled to the Yankees to surrender and come over. Strange to say the two cowards dropped their muskets and gave themselves up as prisoners of war. Swain was the name of one of our boys, but the other I do not remember.

May 17

Same

I spent most of this day with the Yankee wounded. They were in a miserable condition. Many of them were several days without having their wounds dressed. I found many whose wounds were complete masses of maggots. There were many Catholics among them, who had formerly belonged to Meagher's* brigade. I heard their confessions, anointed some, called the attention of the surgeons and nurses to their wounds and aided in washing and dressing some.

May 19

May God grant that I may never again experience such sensations or witness such scenes as I this night felt and beheld. We passed over the ground enclosed in the angle where Grant broke through our lines on the morning of the 12th. The thousands of Yankees slaughtered on that memorable morning are lying there decomposed and unburied. The ground is low and swampy. The atmosphere is densely impregnated with the offen-

---

* Brigadier-General Thomas Francis Meagher, U.S.A. He commanded a brigade of volunteers.

sive effluvia of the dead bodies of men and horses. The sights are shocking. The smell is still more offensive. We are moving through a dense sea of corrupted atmosphere. I became faintish. Doctor Martin,* my immediate companion, complained of being similarly affected. Fortunately he brought with him a flask of brandy, a small portion of which enabled us to bear up under the offensive pressure.

May 20   Morning clear and pleasant; send back our wounded. Visit Doctor Black's** receiving hospital and hear the confessions of some of our men and administered the Sacrament of Extreme Unction. Spend the most part of the afternoon and early part of the night with the Yankee wounded. Have some of them sent back to Richmond and give some who were very weak the last of my Mass wine.

May 21   The surgeon of our regiment had followed the brigade this morning so there was no one to see after these poor fellows but myself. We had a great many empty ambulances. I asked Doctor Stephen† to let these men ride. He told me they might follow after and if they should break down then they might get in. I thought this was too hard treatment for men who were always at their post. I insisted on the men being carried but the doctor would pay no attention to what I said but rode off rapidly. The ambulances followed and left our brave but broken-down soldiers to shift for themselves or fall into the hands of the Yankees.

---

* Joel Martin, assistant surgeon.
** Probably Assistant Surgeon Allen Jackson Black.
† In the Confederate Register there is listed no "Doctor Stephen." There was a William Stephenson, assistant surgeon from December 3, 1863 onward; and a Hennel Stevens was medical storekeeper in 1862. (The question might be raised as to whether every member of the Medical Corps mentioned by Father Sheeran held a medical degree and was therefore technically a "Doctor.")

As was usual the doctor again lost his way and about dark we were near driving into the enemy's lines. We had to change our course and turn towards Hanover Junction. I know not how far we travelled this night but it was one of the most fatiguing of my life. Being pretty well worn out by the almost incessant labors of the last 2 or 3 weeks I was near giving out this night. Sleep had overpowered me. A thousand times was I tempted to tie up my horse and sleep in a fence corner. Being no longer able to remain on my horse without exposing myself to a fall I dismounted and led my old grey. This was no better. I soon fell asleep while walking and was in danger of being tramped by my horse or run over by our wagons. Mounting again I continued my journey, suffering increased misery till about 10 o'clock in the evening when we came up with our brigade camped in a field.

Our wagoners and hospital nurses immediately commenced cooking supper but, although without food from early the morning before, I threw myself on the ground and slept till daylight. Upon awakening almost my first thought was of those poor men left behind. I was satisfied they fell into the hands of the enemy. I repaired to Colonel York and told him in the presence of the doctor how he had treated our men. The doctor throwing himself back on his dignity told me that it was his concern to see after the men, and when I should be appointed surgeon I might then interfere in such matters.

"Doctor," said I, "it is *your place to see* after our men but not to neglect them, and I shall this day report you to the corps commander and if you give me any impudence even to General Lee. I will let you see that you cannot sport with the interests of the service." "I had no empty ambulances," said he. "You had, sir, and you carried your own favorites in them." Our own surgeon came up and said the fault was his, for he should have waited and sent after the men of his regiment. I told him his fault was one of forgetfulness, but that of my dignified friend was one of the will.

After the battles of the Wilderness and Spotsylvania Grant kept driving southward, Lee slowly fell back with occasional sharp flurries forward, and, on June 3, came the murderous clash at Cold Harbor. In this battle Grant's advance was not stopped, but the price Lee made him pay for his progress was terrific. In terms of the larger strategic picture however, Lee was retreating to the Richmond defenses.

Now begins the episode of Early's Raid, a thirty-three-day march that took a Confederate brigade around the right flank of the Federal army and to within three miles of Washington. Father Sheeran accompanies this expedition and, as it returns to Virginia, gives a summary of its accomplishments. He is writing on July 19 from a camp on the Shenandoah river about fifteen miles east of Winchester. The brigade has just recrossed the Potomac and is on its way again southward:

We left the breastworks at Richmond on the 10th of June and since that time have marched over 700 miles driving Hunter* and his Yankee robbers from before Lynchburg into the mountains of Western Virginia, then turned our course through the Valley, capturing an immense amount of supplies consisting of flour, oats, corn, dry goods, sutlers' shoes, horses, wagons etc. After resting there for one day we crossed the Potomac, drove the Yankees from Harpers Ferry, capturing a good amount of supplies there, and destroying all we could not carry away. Our cavalry penetrated Pennsylvania, supplied themselves with good horses and other necessaries, whilst our infantry crossed the South Mountain and captured the city of Frederick and levied a con-

---

* Brevet Major General David Hunter, U.S.A.

tribution of two hundred and fifty thousand dollars on the inhabitants of that city.

We next met the enemy and whipped him well at the Monocacy Junction on the Baltimore pike, three miles from Frederick. Only Gordon's* division was engaged in this truly brilliant affair. We took six hundred prisoners, killed some 150, driving the remainder before us like so many sheep. Our cavalry pursued them towards Baltimore, cut the railroad between Philadelphia and Baltimore and that between Baltimore and Washington, and went within some two miles of Baltimore. Our infantry took the Washington pike and after a rapid march arrived before the Federal capital on Monday afternoon, the 11th of July.

We immediately surrounded the city, cut off all its communications with the Maryland side and our sharpshooters drove every Yankee behind their breastworks. On Tuesday afternoon the enemy, no doubt being largely reinforced, advanced from the breastworks in three lines of battle. Our sharpshooters fell back drawing the Yankees after them for about 800 yards, then suddenly turning upon them charged with a Confederate yell. The scene was now a most amusing one: the Yankees took to their heels, our boys pursued them and when the former were entering their breastworks a tremendous volley from sixteen pieces of artillery added to their velocity.

That night we fell back from Washington and on the next night crossed the Potomac at or near Leesburg. The Yanks thinking no doubt we were falling back through fear followed after us closely with cavalry, but our boys turned on them and gave them a good whipping. We

* General John B. Gordon, C.S.A.

halted at Leesburg and took a day's rest in order to
give the men an opportunity of washing, etc. We resumed our march and crossed the Blue Ridge at a place
called Schnecker's Gap and camped in our present position on the banks of the Shenandoah. Yesterday afternoon the enemy made his appearance in large force.
Our boys soon made preparations to receive them.

The suddenness of the original decision to make the raid is suggested
by a conversation between the chaplain and General Early on one of the
first days of the march:

June 29   About 9 a.m. I met General Early standing in front
of the hotel [at Harrisonburg]. "Well, General," said I,
"I have a grave complaint to make for the manner in
which you have treated me. You took us out of the
breastworks at Richmond, never told us where we were
going and the consequence is I left without money or
clothes, only what I had on my back, and since I have
had to live on the charity of my friends." "I guess, Father, you are better off than I am. I brought with me
but one pair of drawers and had to do without [them]
whilst they were being washed. And my adjutant general had but one shirt and he had to go to bed to get
it washed. So I think there are people worse off than
you, Father."

During the "raid" there had been some incidents deemed worthy of
mention in the diary. At the spectacular Natural Bridge, a few miles
south of Lexington, some of the marching men were allowed to make
a detour in order to enjoy this sight-seers' item (June 24). At Lexington,
the brigade paused to pay its respects to the grave of Stonewall Jackson:
"It was a solemn scene as we marched past the grave with uncovered
heads and slow pace. I saw by the countenances of our men that they
were deeply impressed. No doubt they remembered the many times the
departed Chief had led them to victory and the long and arduous marches
in which they followed him" (June 25). On the way to Winchester the

chaplain, riding near the front of the column, and not being recognized by the men, was greeted by the jeer, "Beggars up front!" (July 2.) He waxes indignant at "our thieving quartermasters" at Martinsburg, who kept to themselves large amounts of the captured stores that should have been given to the men (July 3). One of the few mentions of the chaplain's horse is evoked by the latter's apparent vanity as Father Sheeran is cheered by the people of Frederick: "My grey appeared to feel proud of the honor paid to his rider, or perhaps was restless to follow his companions just gone ahead. From his prancing and jumping about one would conclude that he was 'putting on airs'" (July 9). Incidentally, being tardy in leaving Frederick, Father Sheeran was almost captured by pursuing Yankee cavalry (July 10). He is appalled at the aftermath of battle around the town:

> On the crest of the hill where our men first attacked the enemy, we saw a regular line of dead Yankee bodies. A little in the rear they were to be seen lying in every direction and position, some on their sides, some on their faces, some on their backs with their eyes and mouths open, the burning sun beating upon them and their faces swarmed with disgusting flies.

July 11   [This is his account of the attack on Washington:] About 3 p.m. we reach within three miles of Washington and their outer fortifications. Owing to fatigue many of our men fell out on the road and go to sleep in the fence corners and other places of shelter, so that when we reached within view of Washington nearly one half of our men were behind. But even with the army thus weakened, had he wished General Early could no doubt this afternoon have entered Washington.

This day General Ramseur* was in advance and now throws out his sharpshooters who soon drive the Yankees inside their own works. . . . From my position this [apparently the following] morning I had a clear view of

---

* Major General Stephen Dodson Ramseur, C.S.A.

the enemy's fortifications of the Capitol, and some other large buildings in Washington. . . . In the afternoon the Yankees send out several lines of skirmishers; our men fall back to draw them [the Yankees] from their works and then turn upon them, killing and wounding a good many and capturing some. . . .

Among the captured were some of the "Sixth corps" from Grant's army. This satisfied General Early that no doubt the object of his mission to Washington was accomplished: to draw their forces from before Richmond. Hence everything now indicates a retrograde movement although an offensive attitude is displayed in front. . . .

Between 6 and 7 p.m. heavy columns of the enemy made their appearance outside of their works and advanced very slowly when our skirmishers fell back in great haste. Colonel Folsom,* commanding a battalion of artillery, had his 16 guns in position and when the Yankee columns or lines were within convenient range, suddenly opened upon and drove them precipitately to their works. At dark our whole column was in motion, and I mounting on an old carrion, joined the cavalcade. We travel all night but slowly and reach Rockville about daylight.

The chaplain had made also a few interesting entries recounting incidents that occurred during the brigade's withdrawal from the environs of the capital:

The marches of the last few days [he was writing on July 14, the brigade having just arrived on the Virginia side of the Potomac, near Leesburg] were rapid, and the fatigues so great, the disposition to steal or capture horses so prevalent and the occasions so tempting that

---

* Colonel Simpson W. Folsom, C.S.A.

not only all our broken down men but even many others were mounted, so that our little army crossing the Potomac this night had the appearance of a demoralized cavalry. The men must now be dismounted and the horses secured for the use of the government. Major Harmon,* our corps quartermaster undertakes the job. He places a guard on all the roads from the ford, giving orders that no mounted soldier should pass unless he was entitled to a horse. It was an amusing thing to see the self-constituted cavaliers try to flank the horses and the boys had to ride again on "Shanks Mare."

July 15   This morning the men were informed that we would rest for the day, or in other words we would not march; it was a regular washday. It is rumored that the Sixth corps is yet following us and trying to occupy the passes of the Blue Ridge to prevent our return to the Valley; still we do not march. Towards evening I hear it rumored in camp that the officers of our division are going to a party given by the ladies of Leesburg. I soon discovered by the preparations of the officers that the rumor was well founded.

I spoke to some of them on the subject and not only disapproved of but denounced such reckless carelessness on the part of commanding officers. I asked a general how did it look when we were in the very face of the enemy to see officers neglecting their command and running around the country to "Fandangoes"? "And would it not be well for you, General, to give our men the liberty of doing as their officers?" I succeeded in breaking up the party and some of the officers who were on their way were ordered back to camp.

---

* Major J. A. Harman, of Ewell's Corps.

July 18   And now our division surgeon, a man of perhaps en-
larged but certainly very confused ideas, has his medical
train in beautiful disorder. His ambulances are running
through the country, while he is off looking for a
hospital or perhaps looking for himself, and his medical
wagons are going where they please. I was with the
latter, anxious to know where our hospital would be
established.

The return march to Richmond now gets under way:

July 23   This day I was very much grieved at the profanity
of officers visiting headquarters. I made an effort to
check it. They apologized but the next moment committed the same fault. I resolved to quit the command
and that night took General York to one side to tell
him of my intention. It came upon him like a thunder
clap. He begged me to reconsider the matter and not
to quit the command after being so long with it. He
told me not to mind such and such ones (referring to
those whom I had rebuked for cursing). "General,"
said I, "I don't blame them so much for I cannot expect
much better of them. But I blame you for you are worse
than they are." "Well," said he, "Father, if you consent
to remain with us, you will never hear another profane
word from me." "You have made such promises before,
General, and you know how you have kept them."
After repeated promises of the most solemn kind that
he would reform on this point I consented to remain,
and I have never since heard a profane word from the
general.

Aug. 4   Having had my horse put away and feeling very
Encamped   tired I spread my oilcloth outside my tent and went
near   to sleep for the night. About 10½ the officers returned,
Shepherds- some of them pretty well "fuddled," and one of them
town   shamefully drunk. He was no less than a colonel, a

very corpulent man riding a large horse. I was now lying on my back and in a kind of slumber. I heard the noise of a horse approaching but anticipating no harm as I was lying close to our tent. Suddenly the foot of a horse is pressed upon my left breast and just as suddenly did I feel the whole weight of the animal and his drunken rider bruising me, as I supposed, into jelly. I thought my last moment had come. A cold chill came over me. The horse continued his journey, his rider knowing nothing of what had happened. I was brought into the tent, and having received some stimulants soon became composed and went again to sleep.

Early's force was advancing down the Valley to threaten Washington. On August 4 Lee, at Petersburg, was preparing to send reinforcements to Early. On August 7 Sheridan was sent by Lincoln into the Valley. Father Sheeran then spent a little less than two weeks in Richmond. On August 26 he was back with the army, now stationed in the vicinity of Winchester; and again during the first part of September returned to the Confederate capital. It was here at Richmond that he learned of the serious Confederate defeat at the so-called battle of Winchester. Sheridan had launched out at Early's force and had badly crippled it. The Confederate leader was forced once more to retreat — for the last time — toward Richmond. Father Sheeran returned at once to the front to attend to the wounded and dying and to do his best to bolster the morale of those who still could fight. He had scarcely arrived at the combat area when he took a resolution which, in the light of after events, was momentous.

Sept. 24   From what I had heard of the battle of Winchester
Near   I knew that a large proportion of the wounded were
Winchester   of our brigade and that of them a good many were
Catholics. I knew too that there would be no priest to attend as Doctor Costello of Harpers Ferry had not been there for more than a year although it belonged to his parish. So after serious reflection I concluded to

try an experiment and ride into the Yankee lines and ask Sheridan for a pass to see after our wounded. I knew it was an informal way of acting, but I thought no general claiming to be a Christian would object to my mission. I remained in Harrisonburg all night but did not rest much for I knew not at what moment Sheridan's army might enter the town. I sent my own horse back with my orderly telling him to keep with the command, and I took with me a Yankee horse captured by General York.

Sunday,
Sept. 25

This morning I was up early, took some breakfast and commenced my experimental journey about 7 o'clock. Having travelled some 7 miles I met with 3 cavalry dressed in Confederate uniform. As they approached me I knew by their appearance that they were Yankees in disguise. One of them halted me and proposed the following questions, "Do you belong to the rebel army?" "No sir, I belong to the Confederate army." "Well, get in here," pointing to where I should go. "No sir, I will not." By this time the disguised Yankee was drawing his pistol on me. Seeing his object I remarked, "You are mistaken, sir, in the opinion you form of me. I am a Catholic priest and wish you to bring me to General Sheridan. I am desirous of going to Winchester to see after our wounded and want a pass from your general."

The man brought me to General Wright,* commanding the 6th corps, now in the advance and gave me an introduction. I soon made known the object of my visit and the general having examined my papers ordered his adjutant to write a pass for myself and horse. General Wright thanked me for the kind manner I treated his wounded at the battle of Kernstown and then rode on.

* General Horatio G. Wright, U.S.A.

His adjutant dismounted to write the pass and appeared anxious to obtain information concerning our army. Handing me the pass he asks, "Are there many of your troops in Harrisonburg?" "I came into your lines, sir, to see after our wounded and not to give military information," was my reply. "Well sir, of course you are not bound to do it." I now for the first time since the war commenced found myself within the enemy's lines.

I need not say that I did not feel myself at home but resolved to put on an independent exterior. The whole Yankee army was now marching in line of battle and indeed displayed a very formidable appearance. Some 3 miles from the front I met General Sheridan and staff on the right of the road. I advanced towards him and was met by his adjutant who being apprised of my business told me General Wright's pass was sufficient. On seeing the strength of Sheridan's army today I was not surprised that he defeated Early's little band. My only surprise was that Early attempted to fight with such odds against him.

Having passed the main body I began to meet large squads of stragglers or broken down men; some of them appeared to be very impudent and asked me many questions. I thought it best to show no fear of them and answered their questions generally in as blunt a manner as that in which they were asked. As I approached Mount Jackson I met a squad of very rough fellows who hailed me. One of them said, "Halloo, old fellow, where are the Johnnies?" I pretended not to understand him and asked whom did he mean. "Why I mean the Johnnies." "I don't know any such people," I said. "Well don't you know where the rebs are?" "Oh, yes, sir, I know where they are. Here is one of them talking to you." After a brief pause he again interrogates,

"Where are the other rebs?" "If you would keep in the front with your companions you would know where they are without asking questions." The chap moved on and left me alone.

As I entered Mount Jackson I met another squad. One of them asked me a question in a very rough manner. I answered, if he would ask a question in a gentlemanly manner I would think about answering it. He then bellows out, "Who the hell are you?" I gave the spurs to my horse and sprang towards him. The fellow took to his heels, his companions laughing heartily at him. This ended my first day's experience within the Yankee lines.

I visited our hospitals here this evening. As it was late I spent but a short time with our wounded, intending to call in the morning. I had much anxiety this night for my horse, lest some of the Yankee "bummers" might steal him.

Sept. 26   Visited the hospitals this morning and heard some confessions. My horse safe. Take breakfast and start for Winchester at 7½. I reached Woodstock about 10½.

I called at all the hospitals on the way down and reached Winchester safely at 7 p.m. after a ride of some 48 miles. The folks at Winchester were agreeably surprised at seeing me again amongst them. My reception was indeed a flattering one. I found Father Bixio* who is now playing Yankee chaplain in company with several Yankee officers.

This Father, who is the pastor of the congregation in Staunton, Virginia, followed us into Maryland last

---

* Father Joseph Bixio, listed in the *Catholic Directory* as being stationed in Alexandria, Pa. The "Pa." may be a misprint for "Va."(?)

summer. It appears he made large purchases or received large presents of goods of various kinds and had them forwarded to Harpers Ferry, expecting to bring them back to the Valley when our army should be returning. But as we came back by way of Leesburg, Father Bixio with his merchandise was left inside of the Yankee lines and remained there some three months during which time he made several unsuccessful attempts to get out. But as Sheridan was about to move up the Valley a circumstance occurred which Father Bixio turned to his advantage.

There was a priest by the name of Leo,* a chaplain of the 9th Connecticut regiment in Sheridan's army, who resigned and returned home. Father Bixio on hearing this told Father Leo that he would act in his place. Now having received a quasi installation he has had boxes, trunks etc. labelled "Chaplain 9th Connecticut regiment infantry" and moves off with Sheridan's army for the sake of getting himself and his merchandise to Staunton. It was in this capacity that I met Father Bixio at Winchester.

Sept. 27   This morning I visited all our hospitals and told our boys I came to stay with them for a while. Never did I see men display more cheerful countenances than they did when I made this announcement. I was waited on today by many of the citizens who invited me to make my home with them.

Sept. 28   This morning we had Mass at 6½ and there were several Federal soldiers present. I gave notice this morning of the object of my mission to Winchester, that I had come to see after *our* wounded but was willing to

---

* No Father Leo is listed in the *Catholic Directory* during the Civil War period.

extend my services to the wounded of the Federal hospitals. If Catholic soldiers of the Federal army wished to call to see me, I had no objection if they would come in a respectful manner, but I wished them to understand that if they came with the intention of instructing me in religion or politics they might expect to be treated as they deserved. In conclusion I requested them if they knew of any sick or wounded who needed my services to let me know and I would freely attend them. I spent the most of the day in the hospitals and was truly edified to see the kindness of the people of this truly patriotic and hospitable place to our wounded.

Sept. 29   Mass at 6½. Bring communion to young Garnier* of the 5th Louisiana, who died in the evening. Visit the hospitals in the forenoon. Called upon by Mr. Avirit,** an Episcopal minister, who introduced me to many of his friends.

Sept. 30   Pay a visit to the hospital. Call on the Provost Marshal to see about having Major Garnier transferred from the Sheridan hospital. Obtain a pass to visit the Federal hospitals at will. Procured shoes for some of our barefooted men.

Oct. 1   The weather is quite cold this morning, reminding us that winter was nigh. On visiting the hospitals I found our wounded suffering much from the cold. Blankets, socks and stoves were in great demand. The Yankee medical director promptly supplied an abundance of blankets. I succeeded in collecting a good number of socks, and the Confederate ladies of Winchester, whose labors on behalf of our wounded entitle them to the

---

* Not listed in Confederate Register.
** Diligent search has not resulted in an identification of this friendly Protestant minister.

grateful thanks of their country, succeeded in procuring some stoves. So towards evening our boys felt much more comfortable.

In my visit through the wards today I found one of our men sinking very rapidly. Poor fellow! He was as low in spirits as in bodily health. Having tried to encourage him I saw the surgeon of the hospital and asked him for the privilege of taking care of the young man, expressing my opinion that all he needed was good nursing. He freely consented. I dispensed with the use of the doctor's medicines and by using such remedies as suggested themselves to me the young man soon recovered.

My attention to this patient soon excited the jealousy of other poor fellows who remarked to some of their comrades that if they could get the same treatment they knew they would soon get better. I soon came to hear this and removed the cause of complaint by waiting on them and bringing them their meals, etc. every day. Indeed I gave them a bad habit, for they would eat nothing of the hospital rations and fretted like children whenever I chanced to send their meals by another.

Sunday, Oct. 2

Mass at 8. A small congregation; recited the rosary after Mass. Visit the hospitals as usual. This evening about sundown Doctor Costello* of Harpers Ferry arrived at Winchester. He came to see after the Catholic wounded but on finding me there resolved to return home the next day. We spent an agreeable evening together.

Visit the hospitals in company with Doctor Costello. He urges me to meet him the next Saturday at Martinsburg, and to remove my objections in regard to a pass

* Father M. Costello.

he brought me to the Provost Marshal in order to obtain one for me. The Provost Marshal refused alleging he had no jurisdiction in my case. The Doctor then repaired to the medical director, to whom the Provost had recommended him. This gentleman treated us very kindly, but said the Post Commander alone gives passes under such circumstances. However he said he would give me a letter of introduction to the Post Commander.

Oct. 5-12   From this day to the 12th of October, I visited the hospitals of the Confederate and Federal wounded. Nothing of interest occurred save an interview with the post surgeon who gave me the letter of introduction to the Post Commandant. On reading the letter which he gave me unsealed I found that he introduced me as a chaplain in the "insurgent" army.

I visited the Doctor, suggesting that he had made a mistake in his letter of introduction. "You make use of the term 'chaplain in the Insurgent Army.' I am chaplain in no such organization. I am a regularly appointed chaplain in the Confederate Army. I came into your lines as such. I have been treated as such by your superior officer, General Wright, and I demand to be treated as such by you." "But, Father, you are insurgent. The Commissioners for the exchange of prisoners have agreed to use the term insurgent in their official correspondence." "But, Doctor, I have made no such agreement with you and I will accept no such title." "Father, I did not intend to offend you. What if I introduce you as the chaplain of your regiment?" "I ask no more, Doctor." So he wrote the letter and introduced me as chaplain of the 14th Louisiana regiment of infantry.

Oct. 12   This afternoon I had a visit from several Catholics of the Federal Army. They were very kind and respectful and promised to come to Mass on the following Sunday. Having returned home from my usual visits to the hospitals I was called to see a Captain Brady* of the 16th Massachusetts regiment now lying dangerously ill at the "Logan House." He had been wounded at the late battle of Winchester, had a leg amputated and two other severe wounds. I found him very low indeed, but after receiving the Sacraments he rapidly recovered and was soon able to be taken home by his brother who came from Boston to wait on him.

Sunday, Oct. 16

Mass at 8. A large congregation. Recite the rosary after Mass. I thought it my duty to speak to the Catholic soldiers present with regard to the conduct of the military authorities during the past week. There is always a swarm of sutlers following the Yankee army, anxious to relieve the soldiers and citizens wherever they go of their surplus change. No sooner had the Feds occupied Winchester than a number of them opened stores and sold to the citizens who purchased freely of such things as they needed.

But this week the Post Commandant issued an order to sell no more goods to citizens without an order from the Provost Marshal. But he did not stop here. He sent out a body of men to search private houses and to take from the people the goods which they had purchased and paid for. In speaking of this matter I admitted the right of the military authorities to make rules for their sutlers and also to punish them for any violations of these rules. But as long as they were permitted to sell goods without restraint the citizens had

---

* Captain Allen G. Brady, with the 17th Connecticut Infantry in 1862. At some point of the war he was attached to the 16th Massachusetts Infantry.

a right to purchase, and to take from them the goods thus paid for was not only unjust but contemptibly mean. I cautioned the soldiers against having anything to do with such goods, captured from these citizens, for they might as well steal the money out of their pockets.

Oct. 19   This morning at daylight we hear the report of artillery up the Valley. At first we supposed it to be a cavalry skirmish but soon the reports become more audible and rapid. At 8 a.m. the Yankee post of Winchester was all excitement; at 9 all was bustle and confusion. Doctors had their horses saddled: sutlers were packing up their goods and everything indicated a hasty move. Still the Rebels could get no information of what was going on. About 10 o'clock artillery drivers with their horses and harness but minus their guns began to block the streets of Winchester; soon every road leading down the Valley was crowded with demoralized stragglers.

The place now presented a scene of intense excitement. The cavalry camped around Winchester are now formed into three lines, extending across the roads leading down the Valley to keep back the stragglers. About 10 a.m. General Sheridan and staff left Winchester for the front. All was suspense till about 3½ p.m. when the thundering of artillery was again heard and continued for about an hour when it gradually died away, never again to be renewed by Early's invincible but exhausted little army. I have seen no published account of this eventful battle but will endeavor to give as accurate a description of it as the information received from many Confederate and Federal soldiers, who participated in it, will permit.

On the night of the 18th Sheridan's legions went to rest, placing out their ordinary pickets and little dreading an attack from Early. For who would suppose that Early with his little squad of 8,000 men would dare attack an enemy of 30,000, now flushed with their recent victories? On the afternoon of the 18th Early's boys had orders to prepare rations and be ready to march at sundown. The appointed hour came and agreeable to subsequent orders every man divested himself of his canteen, tin cup, or any other article likely to make the least noise.

Immediately before daylight a signal gun from our extreme left announced that Rosser* had got in position with his cavalry to guard our left flank. The signal had no more been given than Gordon with his small division crossed the Creek, captured the Yankee pickets and swept around the left of the 8th corps, arousing the Yankees from their slumbers by the discharge of their musketry. Now commences a scene which our men tell me beggars description. The camp was soon aroused to a sense of their condition; and jumping suddenly from their beds some seize their pants and boots and made off with their jibs flying before a stiff breeze occasioned by the rapidity of their motion, and others made for their muskets. On the right, whilst this was going on, Early opens his artillery from the heights across the Creek on the 19th corps; then his infantry charges across the ford into the camp and now begins another stampede like that of the 8th corps. In about half an hour our little band had possession of the camps of the 8th and 19th corps and an immense amount of spoils.

Soon General Gordon** got a few batteries in position

---

* Major General Thomas L. Rosser, C.S.A.
** Major General John Brown Gordon, C.S.A.

and swept the plains to the right of the Pike. Here General Wright, who was in command of the Yankee forces, endeavored to rally his forces but in vain for our boys pressed closely after them, strewing the ground with the dead and wounded. Now General Gordon asks permission to charge the 6th corps, which is camped higher up the Creek, but this Early would not permit. His reasons for refusing are not known. The 6th corps seeing the condition of the other corps began to fall back so that by 8 a.m. our boys had driven the enemy nearly 4 miles, captured some 2,000 prisoners, 38 pieces of artillery, immense quantities of provisions, and a large amount of blankets, overcoats, and other winter clothing.

The spoils captured proved a curse to our little army. Seeing the enemy flying before them, instead of joining their brave companions in the pursuit, many now fell out of the ranks and began to plunder so that when they reached Middletown Early's army was reduced to a mere skeleton. Here he discontinued the pursuit in order to rally or collect his scattered troops. This was an unfortunate event for instead of collecting his troops many more betook themselves to plunder, and to their great dishonor be it said, several officers thought more of plundering than of defeating the enemy.

From 9 a.m. to 2 p.m. the portion of Early's army which remained at their post were busy throwing up breastworks whilst our quartermasters and commissaries were occupied in sending back the captured wagons and ambulances. We were unable to remove the artillery as the riders ran off with the horses. We had but few killed or wounded, whilst the enemy's loss in killed and wounded up to this time must have amounted to between 4,000 and 5,000. Our surgeons were busy in caring for them.

This was the state of affairs when Sheridan arrived in the field. His 6th corps was yet intact and he succeeded in rallying a considerable number of the 8th and 19th corps. These he marshalled in the rear of a deep wood lying between his line and Early's. At 3½ p.m. he appeared in line of battle advancing his left, but our artillery open upon them with telling effect and compel them to recoil. Here, as I was told by one of the couriers, Sheridan was near losing his life by a piece of a shell. He next endeavored to advance his right but with no better success. Now the infantry come in close combat and for over an hour a handful of the brave Confederates keep at bay the solid Yankee columns.

Repeatedly Sheridan massed his cavalry on our flanks but our artillery always repulsed them until the ammunition of the batteries on our right gave out. The enemy perceiving this made another charge and got in the rear of our right wing. Our infantry noticing our artillery making to the rear became panic-stricken and now commenced a shameful rout. Our medical wagons and ambulances with our wounded and artillery were making to the rear but unfortunately there was but one road and it narrow, running along a deep ravine. On a stone bridge crossing a stream in this ravine our artillery was blocked up and the whole train literally jammed together. In their efforts one to pass the other, wagons and ambulances were broken in pieces and many of the wounded thrown down the precipice or crushed to death under the wheels of the broken wagons. A few Yankee cavalry captured all this train and about 1,100 of our men as prisoners. Thus ended a battle brilliantly conceived and for a time daringly executed, promising a most splendid victory, but which was lost by the plundering propensities of the otherwise brave and excellent soldiers.

The loss of the enemy in the whole engagement in killed, wounded and missing was between 6,000 and 7,000 whilst the Confederate loss did not reach to 2,000, some 1,600 of them being prisoners. The enemy recaptured the most of their artillery and some of ours. We however succeeded in getting off more of their wagons and ambulances than they captured from us.

Although the material loss of the enemy far surpassed ours, the moral effect was in their favor. They felt themselves masters of the situation in the Valley and boasted loudly of their victory although the piteous lamentations of their 4,000 and 5,000 wounded, with any other people, would occasion sadness and humiliation. But the loss of life appeared nothing; victory over a brave enemy was all they wanted.

Oct. 20   Today there were wild reports from the front; some said that Sheridan was pursuing Early, but the truth is Sheridan was so roughly handled yesterday that his infantry did not advance a 100 yards in pursuit. His cavalry, however, followed the Confederates to watch their movements. Early retreated up the Valley to return no more. Where he fell back I do not know as I am now within the enemy's line and cut off from all communication with our troops. This afternoon large numbers of the enemy's wounded came in, and preparations are made for the reception of 5,000. Some of our convalescent were sent down to Martinsburg. . . .

Oct. 29   General Sheridan is in town and visits all the hospitals. As the most of our men were now sent off and few of our own men needed my services I resolved to see

General Sheridan in order to know by what route he wished me to return home. I called at the headquarters of Colonel Edwards,* where the General was staying, and an officer, whom I afterwards recognized to be the general himself, asked me what I wanted and who I was. I told him my name and expressed a wish to see the General. He told me to see his adjutant, at the same time closing the door in my face. Anticipating some rough treatment I thought it best to defer my visit to Monday and then bring a witness with me, so I took my departure. An officer soon followed me, asking my name and residence which I gave him.

A large drove of milch cows stolen up the Valley pass through Winchester for Martinsburg, and a squad of Irishmen went as an escort with these stolen cows. They, feeling ashamed of being the drivers of these animals stolen from the poor people of the Valley, made out to lose a good many of them on their way, but succeeded in losing them at such places as other poor people could find them. This they told me on their return.

Oct. 31   This morning at 9 a.m., accompanied by Captain Fitzgerald** of the 17th Pennsylvania Cavalry, I went to the headquarters of General Sheridan. The Captain introduced me to the Adjutant general of the Post. I asked him if I could see General Sheridan. He told me to take a seat and he would see. Ten minutes later the adjutant returned with an armed guard, and told him to take me to the Provost Marshal. This I thought a singular proceeding, but as I knew not what disposition they intended making of me I was anxious to have Captain Fitzgerald go with me, but this the adjutant

---

* Brevet Lieutenant-Colonel John Edwards, U.S.A.
** Captain John Fitzgerald, U.S.A. Born in Ireland.

would not permit "for I was a d——d old Catholic priest."

I now found myself for the first time under a Yankee or any kind of guard. The soldier who guarded me appeared to be somewhat ashamed of this work in which he was now engaged. He remarked to me going along, "I will not guard you. You can walk along to the Provost office and I will meet you at the door. I don't see why they should do anything to you. I see you every day at our hospitals attending to our men. I don't know what they will do next." As I reached the door of the office a crowd of citizens assembled to know what Sheridan intended doing with me. I was soon handed over to the Marshal who, on reading the note handed him by my guard, called for his orderly and told him to take me to the military prison.

I asked what charges were preferred against me. "I must obey orders." "Well, sir, I will employ the liberty of my tongue in denouncing my arrest as a mean, cowardly, contemptible, base and treacherous act. I came into your lines with a pass from one of your major generals and now in violation of it I am deprived of my liberty and about to be cast into a dirty prison." He told me that was not his business; he must obey orders and could not discuss these matters.

I was soon ushered into an old building where I found some of the most respected citizens of Winchester, among them several feeble old men averaging from 60 to 80 years, and some of the most vile characters of the Yankee army confined for criminal offences. The good citizens sympathized with me, whilst the latter tried to ridicule me by their rough and vulgar jests. I soon made the latter a little more respectful by a few very cutting remarks.

Captain Fitzgerald and some other officers came to see me to know what could be done for my release. I told them not to trouble themselves about the matter as I was willing the affair should take its course. In a short time several of the Confederate ladies of Winchester asked permission from the Provost to see me but this was refused. One of them was determined not to be put off in this way so she came up to the prison door and asked the guard where I was. Seeing her disposed to come in he demanded her pass. She replied in a determined tone that she needed no pass and as she spoke these words walked into the prison. She wanted to know if I stood in need of anything, or if I would not permit her or her sister to bring me my meals. I thanked her very kindly but refused her kind offers, as I knew the lady with whom I boarded would supply me with the things I might need.

It was a sad sight to see the number of old men confined in this dirty prison and under what charge they knew not. I had many other visitors this afternoon but they were permitted to come no further than the door. One kind friend brought me a few blankets. About 4 p.m. Doctor Robinson,* now post surgeon, came in to see me. He wanted to know the cause of my arrest. I could give him none, but I availed myself of this occasion to denounce the base perfidy of the military authorities and recounted to him what I had done for their wounded soldiers and prisoners. He expressed his sorrow in seeing me treated so, but supposed that General Sheridan did not know about my case. I differed with him for I thought he did. "Well, sir, I can sympathize with you for I was a prisoner at Savannah and I shall never forget the kindness of the Catholic clergy

* Dr. John Milton Robinson, from Ohio.

of that place. And now, sir, in acknowledgement of their kindness I make to you the offers they made to me. Tell me what I can do to contribute to your comfort. If you wish I will supply you with a mattress and blankets and with regard to rations you can have anything you want. If you wish you can have an orderly and you can send him to me for anything you may desire. Perhaps you may be sent away from here, and as your money will be of no value outside of your lines I will cheerfully supply you with all you want."

"Thank you, doctor," said I. "I appreciate your kind offer and will gratefully remember it but I cannot accept it. I have been arrested and sent into this filthy place in violation of the safe conduct signed by a major general of your army. I am determined to put up with prison fare and see how they will treat me."

Just as it was getting dark an officer came into the prison. He told me he would take the responsibility upon himself of letting me go home for the night but as a matter of form he would send a Catholic boy of his company with me so that if called to account he could say that I was under guard all night. During the evening several soldiers came to see me and expressed much indignation at how I was treated.

Nov. 1   About 8½ this morning I returned to prison and found the number of inmates increased by some respectable citizens and one drunken Yankee soldier who was indulging in the most vulgar and blasphemous language. Fearing lest he might possibly be ignorant of my arrest I wrote a letter to General Sheridan and sent it by an officer who assured me that General Sheridan received it.

There are several Confederate prisoners here who have

had nothing to eat for 24 hours. Today the weather is quite cold. The windows are all broken and having no fire we do not feel a bit comfortable, but I tried to keep up spirits as much as possible. About noon a Mrs. Hassett and another lady brought me a very good dinner and an abundance of it. I was somewhat indignant when these ladies were compelled to stand at the prison door till I had finished my dinner. I shared it with some of the Confederate boys.

Nov. 2   One pitiful sight presented itself at the prison door this morning. A poor man living in the environs of Winchester and having a wife and six small children was arrested and is now in prison. His wife near her confinement, after vainly supplicating the authorities, for her husband's release, comes to the prison door bathed in tears and in an almost fainting condition asking her husband what was to become of herself and children, for they had neither firewood nor food. The poor man told her that God alone could tell. He could do nothing for them unless she could obtain his release. This was more than I could stand, so I turned aside from the painful scene.

The citizens are all in commotion today as Sheridan who is seemingly proud of his desolating march through the Valley, now orders the arrest of every citizen of Winchester. Many additions are made to the prison list this afternoon. Even many of those contemptible creatures who either [were] intellectually blind and could not see the justness of the Southern cause, or so servile and mean as to take sides with the enemy against their own State, were imprisoned today. I must confess that I was not one bit sorry for them, and this they could easily perceive.

I was permitted by the officer of the guard to go home for the night although he told me he was exposing himself to punishment for doing so. I wrote a letter to Mr. McMaster of the New York Freeman's Journal and enclosed a copy of my letter to General Sheridan who has as yet not condescended to notice it.

Nov. 3   Return to prison this morning and kept under close guard all day. Many more arrests are made. The weather is cold, making our quarters a little more uncomfortable. Many of the citizens and myself spent the day as cheerfully as possible. None were permitted to leave the prison tonight, and I was honored with a guard even when attending to unavoidable calls.

Nov. 4   I slept little during the night as we had some noisy companions, and if we had not, small animals supply for their absence. I heard the rain falling and also the rumbling wagons during the latter part of the night. About half an hour before day an officer entered the prison and called aloud, "Be up, men, and fall in for roll call." This was an unexpected command but it had to be obeyed. Soon with unwashed faces and half opened eyes we were in ranks to answer to our names. The "roll" being called he ordered us to be ready to march in ten minutes. I asked him where we were going to march to and he replied, "Martinsburg."

"Well, sir," said I, "why did you not give us notice last night so that we might prepare some clothes and provide some breakfast?" "I am obeying orders, sir." "Well, I tell you plainly I shall not go to Martinsburg or to any other place till I go to my boarding-house for my clothes." A soldier seeing I was determined in what I said, told the officer he would accompany me and be responsible for my safe return.

I went for some under-clothing and bade the family goodbye. They were sorry I could not remain for breakfast, but made me take some bread and butter in my haversack.

After a rough and fatiguing ride of 22 miles and with an aching and a somewhat empty stomach I reached Martinsburg about 4½ p.m. On our way from the wagon yard to the Provost Marshal I related to the officer in charge how I had been treated. He kindly offered to do me what service he could. On reaching the office I introduced myself to the Provost and gave him a brief history of my treatment. He looked at the list of prisoners sent from Winchester and then told me, "Sir, I find no charge against you." "Well, captain," said I, "I do not feel well and if I have to sleep in an exposed place tonight I fear my health will suffer." "Well, I will take it on myself to parole you for the night."

Nov. 5   Report at the office of the Provost at 8. Finding him something of a gentleman, I told him I felt it my duty to say Mass on Sunday, and if it would not put him to any inconvenience I would like to remain in Martinsburg for that purpose. "I have to send you to Baltimore. Can you not say Mass there?" "If I were free I could, but I do not know whose hands I may fall into there. Since my arrest you are the only gentleman I have found among the Federal officers and it may be that I shall be equally unfortunate for the future." I found these remarks pleased him, although they were not compliments to his brother officers. After a moment's reflection he replied, "Well, report when you please."

So now by the very kind permission of a Yankee officer I have the liberty of a city, through which I in company with our brave Confederates often before marched in triumph. I visited some warm friends today and received many marks of kindness. Many called upon me at the doctor's and insisted on my accepting some "greenbacks" as I would need them in prison. I thanked them but told them I had friends in Baltimore who would supply all my wants. No refusal would be taken. I had to accept the donation.

Sunday,
Nov. 6

Hear some confessions this morning. Say Mass at 8 o'clock, have a good number present and preach a short sermon. Called at the Provost Marshal's office. He tells me to "call again tomorrow." Many of the poor people shed tears when hearing of the treatment I had received, for many of them knew of my kindness to their wounded.

Nov. 7

Report at the Provost Marshal's office. I found the Provost very busy, so I had to remain some two hours during which time I had an opportunity of seeing the *modus operandi* of a Provost in the discharge of his official duties. I heard perjury enough that day to damn a nation. As soon as he was disengaged he paroled me again till the next day.

Nov. 8

Report this morning and the Provost told me to return about 11 as he would have transportation for me and the other prisoners at that time. At the appointed hour I reported and fell into ranks with some 50 other prisoners now on their way to Baltimore. The Provost in giving the list of prisoners to the guard told him he might not trouble himself about me on the way, and that he should tell the Provost in Baltimore that there were no charges against me and that he thought I should be dismissed.

We now started from the Old Court House to the depot along a very muddy street and with all eyes upon us. We reached the depot, not exactly mud to the eyes but mud to the knees. Here we had to wait two long hours as the train from the West was that much behind time. Before me in a government yard I saw a number of our ambulances captured at the battle of Cedar Creek.

We reached Baltimore about 7 p.m. and were marched to the Provost Marshal's office. I had hoped that the Provost Marshal would have paroled me for the night but how sadly disappointed! We were led into the office in single file, and soon formed a line in front of an individual whom I first thought to be the Provost Marshal. Our guard handed him the list of our names and other papers, informing him at the same time who I was and that there were no charges against me. Then he remarked that he was not the Provost Marshal but would consult him on the subject. He retired and after a few moments' absence informed me that the Provost ordered me to be placed with the rest.

He on giving me this information said he was sorry, but I should have patience and he would see what could be done for me by and by. Then turning to my fellow-prisoners he remarked, "Gentlemen, you are going among a hard crowd tonight. We have pickpockets and some of the very hardest cases. If you have anything about you of value, you had better give it up for you will certainly have your pockets picked."

After the searching operation was concluded we were led into a dark yard, then up a dilapidated stairs without railing, outside of an old brick building, then into a dark room the stench of which was offensive beyond expression. "There are four rooms here, gentlemen," he said, "and you can locate yourselves wherever you please."

The former inmates now occupied in gambling in the other room on hearing us, rushed out to where we were, calling aloud, "Fresh fish! Fresh fish!" They were the hardest-looking specimens of humanity I had ever seen. The poor citizens along with me were somewhat alarmed, but I thought it best to put on an independent exterior. My companions seeing this became partially composed and the rowdies withdrew to their quarters. Having procured a light we sought out what appeared to be the cleanest and most comfortable spot for our bed, or for our oil cloths, as we had no beds. What scenes of filth! The joints of the boards in the floor were full of grey backs, the walls were lined with them, and a water-closet nearby was ejecting its filthy contents.

We had hardly laid our wearied bodies down on the hard, filthy and vermin-covered floor than the former inmates of this institution, inspired as it were by the devil, commenced what appears to be their regular nocturnal exercises. They first had a quarrel, real or pretended, in which vulgarity, obscenity and profanity, such as I never before had heard, were exhibited. Then names, surpassing anything to be found in vocabulary or billingsgate were applied to each other. One would burst out with some verse or phrase of an obscene or vulgar song. Soon another would begin to grunt like a hog and others to bark like a dog, another quack like a duck, another to crow like a cock, another to mew and spit like an angry cat.

It is needless to say that I slept none, for who could sleep? The vermin that had now introduced themselves to us and were exacting tribute of our blood, cost us little concern, for the vulgarity, profanity and obscenity were such as to render all other afflictions of very little consideration. However, towards morning the nocturnal tormentors fell asleep and gave us a few hours peace.

Nov. 9   Today as morning dawned, we repaired to the yard in hopes of getting a little fresh air, but our hopes were not realized for the yard is not more than 20 feet square and is surrounded by a wall as high as the yard is long. We found ourselves in the old "Slave Pen," so notorious in Baltimore. Soon a squad of Confederate prisoners, who had taken the oath of allegiance, made their appearance in our yard with a large kettle of coffee and a very big basket of bread and pork. Some of these fellows recognized me, and feeling ashamed of what they had done told me the motives they had in taking the oath: to join the Yankee army and desert to the Confederates. I did not approve of their conduct but said little to them. Seeing they had the distribution of the rations I exhorted them to be kind to our citizen-prisoners from Winchester as they had placed me under many obligations to them for their kindness. I need not say that they were well supplied with coffee, bread and pork during our 3 days' sojourn at the "Slave Pen" of Baltimore.

During the day the former inmates of the prison appeared to behave themselves better. I asked one of them concerning his religion and he told me he had been brought up a Catholic. I then asked him how it was possible he could have behaved himself as he did last night. He declared that he did not know who I was, or he would not have acted so. I then had him call his companions together and after giving them a severe lecture they promised to behave themselves better for the future. I told them I did not wish to deprive them of harmless recreation and if they wished to play a game of cards for amusement I would not object, but there must be no swearing; at 9 o'clock the lights must be out and all go to rest. They promised and indeed kept it pretty well. At half past nine they were engaged in a game, but on my going into their room and showing them by my watch that the time had expired they threw up the cards, extinguished the lights and retired to rest. Were it not for the stench of the water-closet and the grey backs who appeared to be making their revolutions on our bodies we might have slept soundly for we were tired and our last night's tormentors quiet. However we slept some.

Nov. 10   This morning the Confederates again brought us our rations and indeed an abundance of them. Some of them had procured cakes and other delicacies for myself and distributed liberally of the coffee, meat and bread to my companions, the citizen-prisoners. Many of these citizens remarked that it was hard to be dragged from their homes, but they were very fortunate in having me with them.

This morning about 9 o'clock another batch of citizen-prisoners of Winchester arrived. Our citizens were much pleased today seeing the comparatively good conduct of the former inmates of the prison. I found today that some of them were destitute of money, so I divided what I had with them.

Nov. 11   It rained all night and the atmosphere was close and damp, rendering the stench of our quarters almost unbearable. We slept little as our grey-backed companions were particularly active during the night; hence we were glad when day came.

About 2 p.m. we received orders to march to Fort McHenry. This was a relief for us, as we expected there better quarters if not more agreeable companions. At 3 p.m. we were escorted by a guard from the "Slave Pen" of Baltimore to be incarcerated in one of the artillery stables of Fort McHenry.

Between citizens and soldiers there were about 50 of us. The distance we had to march is about two and a half miles, but to me that afternoon it appeared almost a day's journey. As we approached the outer gate of the Fort there were many poor women selling fruit and other things. These soon observed me and many exclaiming, "There is a priest. Oh, what will they do next when they are imprisoning priests now!" Several of these poor women approached and offered me some apples, but they were driven off by the guard. The officer commanding our escort having presented our credentials and they being found "all right," we were admitted to the prison yard and the massive iron gate soon secured us.

Convenient to Fort McHenry there are three old stables formerly occupied by the horses of the United States Army stationed at the Fort. These stables are about 80 feet long 20 feet wide, the upper story being formerly occupied as a hay-loft. They are running parallel with each other and about 80 feet apart. There is a plank fence about 12 feet high extending around the three buildings and near the top is a platform on which guards are placed and from which they can see all that passes in the interior yards. Besides this outer fence there are others about ten feet high surrounding each stable.

Each stable is divided by a plank partition in the middle, leaving 4 apartments in each, and the yards are again subdivided to correspond with the division of the stables. Those who were incarcerated in the lower part of the stables had a yard 40 feet by 40, whilst those on the hay loft had no yard at all. In each of these apartments there were from 80 to a 100 prisoners. The officer from the Provost introduced us to one of these little yards and then left us to seek our own lodgings.

We had scarcely entered when a crowd of spectators flocked to the doors and windows of the adjacent building curious no doubt to see the new visitors. I viewed the surrounding scene for some moments in silence. I saw among the spectators all classes of society and could recognize some old acquaintances. In the apartment to which I was consigned were Federal prisoners serving out their sentence.

The interior of this stable prison presented a dismal and most filthy aspect. There was but one door and one window which was in the extreme end. Besides these there were other long apertures at the sides of the stables where the horses used to stand. On each side of the stable there was a platform or floor raised some 5 inches from the main floor in the centre. On this platform the prisoners spread their blankets if they had any and spent their nights, I will not say slept, for our poor citizens were afraid to sleep because there were so many pickpockets who went around at nights cutting the pockets of those whom they suspected of having any money.

The posts which formerly divided the stalls are yet standing and serve as the supports of another platform raised some 4 feet from the ground. These were also used as sleeping apartments. On one of these platforms at the extreme end of the building they had already fixed up a bunk for me and as I entered they kindly led me to my quarters and I gave my bunk the title, "Stall No. 1" from which I dated all my subsequent letters. I soon discovered that the stable of Fort McHenry bore some relation to the "Slave Pen" of Baltimore. It was alive with vermin. There were about 80 prisoners crowded in this abode of filth.

As I have remarked there were all classes of society represented: Negroes, Federal soldiers, Confederate gentlemen from the Valley of Virginia, some of them near 80 years of age. They were dragged from their houses without any charges or even a moment's notice and we had even a Methodist preacher. In the next apartment to us were confined those desperate characters known as "bounty Jumpers." These aided by a few of the same class in "our house" succeeded in opening a passage between the two apartments by removing a plank and replacing it again without the knowledge of the Provost. Some of the citizens told me that these rowdies used to come in at night and cut the pockets of those they found sleeping, and that they were afraid to complain of them lest they might take their lives, for some of them had made threats to that effect.

It may be imagined how uncomfortable I felt in my new residence. But there was something yet more painful and revolting than all this. All feelings of delicacy and laws of modesty were entirely ignored. A pit, dug in the middle of the yard where one was exposed not only to the view of the inmates of our own apartment but to the prisoners of the surrounding buildings, was the only place of retirement. Any and everything else I could bear but this was too revolting. I sent for the Provost and protested against it. He said he was sorry but could do no better for me.

Nov. 12   This morning a fellow evidently well-versed in profanity, came into our prison calling out, "You d——d bushwackers, turn out, turn out for roll call." Soon all were in ranks and answered to their names. Next we heard resound through the prison the cry "breakfast" and soon all made for their tin cups etc. The prison fare for the Federal prisoners consisted of plenty of "hard tack" and good coffee for breakfast, hard tack and about half a pound of pork for dinner, and plenty of coffee and bread for supper. The citizens and Confederate prisoners received but two hard crackers three times a day and a small portion of meat for dinner. Of course they had an abundance of water.

There were about 7 or 8 Irish Catholics of the Yankee army confined with us. These poor fellows used to succeed in procuring enough of coffee to divide with me and several of the citizens from the Valley. Besides this we were permitted to make purchases from a sutler so that after all, if we had money, we could live. Today I wrote to the New York Freeman's Journal, dating my letter from "Stall No. 1, Military Stables, Fort McHenry." On the receipt of my letter Mr. McMaster publishes the . . . account of my arrest and also my letters to General Sheridan and my letter to himself from Winchester.

Military Prison, Winchester, Va.

My Dear Mr. McMaster. — The correspondents of the public press have given glowing, if not very accurate accounts of General Sheridan's Victories in the Valley. They have detailed minutely the number of rebels killed or prisoners taken, and of artillery captured. They have heralded to the world, even without a blush of shame for disgraced humanity, the number of barns, and of wheat and hay stacks burned, of houses plundered, of families impoverished and left without shelter or food — but there is one brave and chivalrous act which I believe no correspondent has yet noticed. On the 25th of Sept., as General Sheridan's army was advancing in line of battle on Harrisonburg, I resolved to enter his lines, and ask for a pass to Winchester, in order to attend to our wounded here. I was brought by a scout to General Wright, who commanded the advance. The General treated me very kindly, and commanded his Adjutant to give me a pass through the lines. I next met General Sheridan and staff, and introduced myself to his Adjutant, asking him for a pass to Winchester. He replied, "General Wright's pass is sufficient."

I called at all the hospitals from Harrisonburg to Winchester, and administered the Sacraments to some wounded soldiers. I reached Winchester, September 26th, since which time to October 31st, I have been daily ministering to the spiritual wants of the wounded of both armies, and doing what I could to aid them in other respects. Being desirous to see Gen. Sheridan on some business, and hearing he was in town, I called at the headquarters of Col. Edwards, commanding post at Winchester, where Gen. Sheridan was staying. To my great surprise, I was not only denied an admittance or audience, but was, by the order of Gen. Sheridan, cast into a dirty prison, the officer who executed his order, saying I was a "d——d old Catholic priest." From my prison I sent the General the following hastily written letter, and as I have as yet received no answer, I am forced to conclude that he endorses the conduct of his subordinate officers.

Let it be known, then, to the Catholics of the United States, that Gen. Sheridan has gained another victory, not over the defenseless women and children of the valley, but by throwing a Catholic priest into a dirty prison to be the companion of drunken and disorderly soldiers, and this, too, when some of his own Catholic soldiers are dying without the sacraments.

James Sheeran,
Chaplain 14th La. Regt., C.S.A.

Military Prison, Winchester, Va., Nov. 1, 1864

Major-Gen. Sheridan. — Dear Sir: — Fearing that you are not aware of the fact that a Catholic Priest has been cast into prison, on, or by command of Col. Edwards, I deem it my duty to make the following statement:

I am a Chaplain in the C.S.A. for the last three years and three months, and have been with the army of Northern Virginia, from the evacuation of Yorktown to the present time. On all the bloody fields of Virginia, Maryland and Pennsylvania, thousands of Catholic soldiers, of both armies, have received the Sacraments of the Church at my hands. Even at the late battle of Kernstown, the lamented Col. Mulligan, and many of his Catholic soldiers were attended by me at their last moments.

Being absent from my command, at the late battles of Winchester, and knowing that many Catholics might die without the Sacraments, I resolved to ask your permission to come and see after the wounded here. I entered your lines near Harrisonburg, and was brought to Gen. Wright who, being satisfied I was what I professed to be, treated me very kindly, and gave me the enclosed pass. I met you and staff advancing through the fields on the right of the road, and told your Adjt-Gen. my business, and asked a pass also of him. He replied that Gen. Wright's pass was sufficient. I continued my journey, and reached Winchester on the 26th of Sept., since which time I have ministered to the spiritual wants of all who called for me, and have attended the sick of your army, as well as of our own.

I am pleased to say that I have received the kindest treatment from the officers and surgeons of Winchester, if I except Capt. ——, Adjt.-Gen. of Col. Edwards. I had occasion to call upon him, in company with another Catholic Priest, and I am sorry to say that the Captain acted in a manner both impertinent and ungentlemanly.

Last Saturday, hearing you were in town, I called at your quarters in order to make known to you my situation here. I was told, in a very rough manner, that I could not see you. Yesterday morning I called at your quarters for the same purpose, when, instead of an interview, a guard was sent for, and I was cast into a dirty prison, in company with drunken and blackguard soldiers, where I now remain.

I make these statements to you, General, not that I ask to be relieved, but that you may understand the state of the case. But I cannot help protesting against my treatment as a violation of good faith and a disregard of the protection given by a Federal general. Should I be retained in prison it will satisfy me that you, General, endorse the conduct of the post commander, and I am satisfied to let the public decide upon the merits of the case.

With much regard for your personal welfare, I remain, General, your humble servant,

James Sheeran
Chaplain 14th La.

Sunday,
Nov. 13

This morning the weather is cold and the air damp. After breakfast I walked for some hours in the yard. It was indeed a sad morning for me. I thought of the folks at home, of the people then no doubt devoutly attending Mass. I could hear the church bells of Baltimore chiming their holiday notes and could imagine our fathers then offering or preparing to offer the Holy Sacrifice. But these reflections only served to increase my own misery. Here I was within half an hour's walk of one of our churches, shut up in a filthy stable, compelled to associate with the vilest of characters, and deprived even of the privilege of assisting at the Holy Sacrifice, denied even the privilege of having a priest call to see me.

About nine o'clock this morning as I was pacing the yard and meditating on my sad condition some few Protestant gentlemen called upon me and asked if I would not "hold service" for them that morning. I told them no, as I had no vestments, altar furniture or vessels. They expressed their sorrow but requested that I should at least make some remarks. After a little reflecting and believing I might effect some good I consented to preach for them.

At the appointed time I ascended the platform and commenced by blessing myself and then explaining for the benefit of the Protestants present the object of making the sign of the cross. I then denounced in very severe terms the vulgar vices of gambling, profanity and obscenity. I reminded them how painful it was for respectable citizens to be dragged from their homes and incarcerated, but how much more painful to be compelled to listen to the language of many of those who were listening to me. I exhorted them to discontinue their obscene and profane language if for no higher reason, at least through respect for their fellow-prisoners. I was much consoled at the effects of my remarks for the prison looked more like a convent the remainder of the day than a conglomeration of classes, professions, and religious denominations. We went to bed at a regular hour this night and all rested quietly for the first time in Fort McHenry.

Nov. 14   The conduct of the men today remarkably good. The citizens are delighted with the improved state of affairs. After dark several parties asked me if I had any objection to their playing a game of cards? I told them no, but the lights must be out at half past nine. The lights were extinguished at the appointed time and all went to rest. Another quiet day had passed.

Nov. 15   Write this morning to Reading, Pennsylvania and send my letter by the "Underground Railroad." My beard is now disgracefully long and I sent an officer to the Provost Marshal to ask permission to go to the barber's shop to get shaved. The Provost sent me back word that I might do without shaving. One of the prisoners shaves me. The men are now uncommonly kind and do all they can to make me comfortable. We have access to the sutler's shop and are living tolerably well.

Nov. 16   The usual prison routine today. After dark I was sent for to the Provost Office. Father Miller* is here accom-

_____
* Father Sheeran's spelling is incorrect. The priest was Father M. N. Mueller, of the Redemptorist Congregation.

panied by the son of General Morris* who is now in command of Fort McHenry. The Father was at Washington to see about my release but had to come back to get a statement of how I came into the Yankee lines, how I was arrested, and how treated since my arrest. I gave in writing a simple statement of these facts.

Nov. 17   No papers are admitted into the prison today and no meat for dinner. A batch of Confederate prisoners arrived at the Fort today. They were taken from hospitals where they had been nursing the wounded.

This afternoon about four I was sent for by General Morris. The general said in a very stern and solemn manner, "Well, sir, I have an order from Washington for your release if you will take the oath." "General, I'll take no such oath nor is it honorable to ask me. I was arrested by a violation of faith and this injury and insult is now offered. I shall take no such oath." "Well, sir," said he, "I can't be your attorney." "I never asked you, general." "Well then you must plead your own case." "I have no case to plead. I am here the victim of perjured faith." "Well, sir, you have to go back to prison." "All right, general. I know the way back."

Nov. 18   This morning the weather is wet and as the men have to keep [to] the house the atmosphere of the prison is most disagreeable. Some 7 Federal prisoners were added to our number today. They are hard cases and seem to pride themselves on their blackguardism. Some of the old prisoners told them that there was a priest present and that they should behave themselves. This seemed to make them worse.

Nov. 19   We have no sutler today. Feel it much as my health

* Brevet Major-General William W. Morris, U.S.A.

is failing and I cannot eat the prison fare. Last night was a most unpleasant one. The newcomers seemed to dream blasphemy for I heard them frequently making use of the most shocking profanity in their sleep. It was one of my most miserable nights. I again rebuked these wretches for their profanity but with no good effect.

Sunday,
Nov. 20

The weather this morning is very cloudy, giving to everything a shade of gloom. After breakfast which was a very frugal one I spent some hours in pacing our not very extensive yard, meditating on the sad changes lately taken place in this country which once boasted so loudly of its love of liberty. A citizen prisoner, a native of Maryland and a Methodist, came and asked me in the name of many other gentlemen if I would not be kind enough to preach for them. I gladly accepted the invitation and now determined to bring the new-comers to a sense of duty.

At the hour of ten all the prisoners, excepting three of the rowdies referred to, took their seats on each side of the prison in regular order. I stood on the platform for some minutes with my eyes fixed on those three fellows now at the door and evidently fixed on mischief. Two of them unable to stand my constant and angry-looking glance slowly moved up and took their seats. But their vulgar and badly-disposed companion became even more intent on mischief, sat down by the stone which was near the door and began to look for *game*. I remained silent and on the platform till I saw this fellow commence his vermin chase; then knowing his object was to insult me and disturb the meeting, I walked down to where he was sitting and fixed my eyes directly on his. My looks must have very forcibly spoken my meaning. Without my even speaking a word the fellow cowed down, put on his shirt, took a seat with the rest and I returned to the platform and commenced my sermon.

I know not where my words or ideas came from on that occasion but it appears to me that I pictured the vices of impurity and profanity in such colors that even the most abandoned would feel ashamed of themselves. I thanked our former companions in prison for their good and improved conduct and contrasted their behavior with that of those who were now shocking our sensibilities by filthy exhibitions of their low vulgarity and profanity. As I finished my sermon all eyes were giving a look of contempt on these low, vulgar wretches. One of them felt ashamed of his conduct and did better, at least for a few days; the other two were more determined than ever to show a dogged disregard for anything decent, moral or honorable.

The usual good order presided today for these fellows generally let loose only after night.

Nov. 21   Last night it would appear as if the evil one had taken full possession of these two unfortunate men of whom I have so frequently spoken. It was sickening me to the very soul to hear their filthy conversation. I knew not what to do for if I should rebuke them it might make them even worse if possible.

Nov. 23   Last night the conduct of these two unfortunate men was insufferable. It would appear as if the devil was inspiring them with peculiarly shocking words to express their most filthy ideas. I was determined if I should survive this extremely long and painful night to make another effort to conquer or reclaim my tormentors. I saw this morning that the Catholic prisoners were very indignant at the conduct of those bad men and were concocting measures to compel them to behave by coercive means. I saw trouble was brewing and so I immediately sent a note to the Provost asking a short audience which was granted.

The Provost received me kindly, and asked my business. "Well," said I, "it is hard enough for me to be deprived of my liberty by being shut up in the old stables of Fort McHenry, but I do protest solemnly against being forced to listen to the profanity and obscenity of those wretches whom you last sent amongst us. Their language is shocking, their conduct insufferable." "Well, father, I am very sorry. I had no idea there was such conduct going on in your quarters. I know they were a hard set before you went there and used to give me a deal of trouble, but it has been remarked and talked of throughout the Fort how well the men were behaving themselves since you came among them." "Captain, I am much edified with the conduct of all my fellow prisoners with the exception of two, but on them neither reason nor kindness can make any impression." "I know," said he, "there were some desperate ones," and he referred to one whom he suspected to be the very leader. "You are mistaken, captain, that young man if he is rough in his character knows how to be a gentleman. Since my first conversation with him he has shown me every mark of respect." "Well, father, I will go into the quarters this afternoon, and without letting them see you, you may point them out to me and I will put a stop to their conduct." "But, captain, why delay to the afternoon or ask me to point them out without letting them see me?" "They are desperate characters," said he, "and I thought you would be afraid of them knowing that you complained of them." "You mistake my character altogether, Captain."

So I brought the Provost with me into the stables. All eyes were upon us for they might easily see I was bent on something. The hard cases looked now as innocent as lambs. All now crowded into the prison and I had some difficulty in discerning my men. At length I saw one of them in an upper bunk, and immediately pointed to him. The fellow putting on a look of innocence asked in the mildest kind of a manner, "What have I done?" "What have you done?" said I. "You had better ask what have I *not* done? Your language is too filthy to be heard. You are a disgrace to the name of a man, and are a fit companion only for the lowest of animals."

The Provost ordered him down and gave him a severe lecture, and on his promising to do better, and at my request, did not inflict any further punishment on him. The Provost then asked where were the others. I soon pointed out the second but he refused to come at the Provost's call, so he grabbed him by the collar, dragged him out of the stable, got a guard, and sent him over to one of the cells of the fort where he places him in what they call "double irons." The Provost gave the men a severe lecture and then turning to me said, "Father, if you hear one of them making use of a profane or obscene expression tell me and I shall show that such things will not occur with impunity."

Nov. 24   Today there was good order in the prison and all seemed thankful that I succeeded in putting an end to the nuisance. My health begins to decline and I can with difficulty keep up my spirits. My heart and head are much affected, the prison fare is very objectionable and the manner of distributing it is much more so.

I believe they selected one of the most contemptible

creatures of the Yankee army to distribute our rations. He with a couple of negroes made their first visit in the morning about 7 with a big boiler of coffee and a box of hard tack. The prisoners had to fall in ranks and then pass by this dignified official and receive their rations as he moved on. If one did not get into ranks he got nothing till the rest were served, and then usually there was nothing left. I had one great objection to getting in ranks: the danger of getting some of my neighbors' stock. Hence I often fell short and came in disagreeable collision with the "grub boss," or the "kitchen wall-paper," as he was called. In the morning he gave coffee to the Federal prisoners but hard tack only to the citizens and Confederate soldiers. At noon he distributed pork not in too large a quantity and hard tack. In the evening about 6, coffee and hard tack to the Federal prisoners but hard bread only to the Confederates.

It was somewhat amusing to see the rush for the tin cups and plates when grub would be announced, everyone endeavoring to be first in ranks. The prison would be for the moment in the wildest confusion. Even old gentlemen of high standing and respectability would join in the race for an advanced position in the ranks for rations. We had in prison with us 8 good Irish boys who would rather remain in prison than fight for the Yankees. These often cheered us by their strokes of wit and by their shrewdness kept me and my citizen friends from the Valley well supplied with coffee; each one of them had a tin bucket and when grub or coffee was announced they were sure to be in the advance of the ranks and get their buckets filled. Having left the coffee near their bunks they would take it to the citizens and again push themselves into the ranks and secure another supply. They sometimes even procured a third supply without being detected. Thus they supplied not only our poor citizens but some of the Confederate soldiers with coffee.

There were a few citizens who were truckling to the Yankee authorities. These fellows had to do without coffee for neither the Federal nor Confederate soldiers would share with them. Indeed they were despised by all.

Nov. 25   This morning the weather is pleasant but I feel quite unwell. The Provost gave orders that no citizen or Confederate will be permitted to make purchases at the sutler's store. Thus we are reduced by the regulations of the prison to hard bread and water and a small piece of meat once a day. This was hard for those who had money and were willing to purchase their own rations. Still our good Irish boys did not permit us to suffer for they had access to the sutler's and bought us what we wanted in their own names. Six other prisoners arrived today from Winchester. Their accounts of Sheridan's treatment of citizens are heart-rending. He is clearing the country of all its male inhabitants, old and young. My health is still sinking.

Nov. 28   Continue unwell. My heart is being much affected. I can with difficulty speak. This afternoon the Provost makes his appearance in the prison for the first time since he deprived us of the privilege of the sutler's store. He seemed in good humor and anxious for a conversation. I thought I should accommodate him and remarked, "Captain, you have for reasons unknown to us deprived us of the privilege of the sutler's store." "O, yes! the sutler was always violating orders by selling to Confederate prisoners." "That is very strange, captain, for you know *she* had been selling to us ever since we came here and you never before objected to it." "It was always against orders, sir." "Well, Captain, I cannot live on the prison fare and I do not see why I should be prevented from having the necessaries of life when I am willing to pay for them." "The prison fare is very good." "I deny it, Captain. I cannot live on it." "Well, I had often to live on worse," said he. By this time we had quite a crowd around us. "I don't doubt you a bit, Captain, but that does not alter the fact. I cannot live on such fare." "The sutler must obey orders," said he. "Surely, then, captain, your government does not intend to murder me by the process of starvation, after depriving me unjustly and shamefully of my liberty." The Captain moved for the door and visited us no more during the remainder of my stay at Hotel Fort McHenry. The boys, however, continued to make purchases for us without Blackjack's knowledge.

As my health is now fast declining and as I see no hope of my release save on dishonorable terms I resolve to write to Secretary Stanton and demand my release or better treatment. I wrote the following letter or note.

Stall No. 1
Artillery Stables
Fort McHenry   November 28th

To the Honorable E. M. Stanton, Secretary of War.

Some twelve days ago I presented to you through a friend a statement of my case. I was then under the impression it was only necessary to make *that statement* to be released from my present painful and certainly uncalled for position. But I was much surprised when instead of an order to have me sent across the lines you ordered General Morris to release "Reverend Sheeran if he will take the oath of allegiance." Now, sir, to take such an oath would require on my part a sacrifice of honor and conscience which I am prepared to make for no earthly consideration. But you say in case I refuse to take the oath I will have "an opportunity to present other papers and evidence." I have, sir, no other papers and evidence and can only repeat what I have already said.

[After explaining the manner of his arrest the letter continues:]

I remember well, sir, the treatment received by the Catholic chaplains of your army, captured at the first battle of Richmond and must say that my treatment within the Federal lines presents a painful contrast. They were permitted to stay at the residence of Bishop McGill* till an opportunity presented itself to send them home. Yet they were prisoners of war, regularly captured, and I came on an errand of charity and with the consent of a Major General of your army.

Now, sir, I request to be sent home and if you have no objection I would like to return by way of Winchester in order to procure my horse and clothing, for General Wright gave me a pass for my horse as well as for myself. Hoping you will attend to my case as soon as time will permit, I am, sir, etc.

Up to this time I had received several communications from friends in Baltimore offering to supply me with anything I might stand in need of. By these means I was able to supply many of the poor citizens with things they much needed.

---

* Most Reverend John McGill, of Richmond.

Among the citizens was a man who had a plantation near Winchester. He was but lightly clad and seemed to suffer some from the cold. He came to me this afternoon and asked me if I could not procure him some articles of clothing from my friends in Baltimore. I told him, "certainly" and asked him what he needed. He answered "underclothing." So I promised to write out for them the first opportunity.

He had no sooner retired than an Irishman belonging to the Federal army came up to me and asked if I knew that fellow. I answered that I knew him only as a prisoner. "Well," said he, "He's a *mane* man and I thought if you knew him you wouldn't bother yourself getting anything for him. He has plenty of money and besides I heard him offer to take the Yankee oath several times since he came here and I also heard him tell the officer he was a good Union man and always done what he could for the Union soldiers about Winchester, whilst he never done anything for the rebels. So, Father, if you knew him you would not get him anything."

That was correct for had I known the fellow I should not have promised anything to him and now I resolved not to keep my promise. After dark as I was sitting in my bunk writing as I usually did my writing after night for there was not light enough in the stable to work in the day time, the man came up to know if I was writing out for those things. I answered him "No, and I don't intend to. You are a Yankee, I understand, and are willing to take as many oaths as they wish to ask you; besides I understand that you have made declarations that you never helped the Confederate soldiers whilst you always helped the Yankees when they were about Winchester. Now, sir, what things I might procure in Baltimore I would ask from my friends for Confederate prisoners, so to ask anything for you would be seeking things under false pretences."

Dec. 1 Remain long in bed this morning, having spent a sick night. I sent to the Doctor's and got some "drops" but they did me no good. Much cast down in spirits. Evidently I cannot stand my treatment long as both food and atmosphere here are affecting me much. The latter is so filthy and dense that it is almost suffocating me, particularly at night as there is no ventilation. I think much of death but care little about it, could I but receive the benefits of the Sacraments.

Sunday, Dec. 4 This morning several Protestant gentlemen expressed a desire to have me preach but I could not. This afternoon about 4 an officer came into the prison inquiring for Reverend James Sheeran. I answered my name as best I could but not in an audible voice for my voice was now nearly gone. Some of the gentlemen brought the officer to my bunk.

He told me he had an order for my release and that I was wanted at the office of the Commissary of prisoners. I remarked, "It is almost time, sir. Had you delayed for a few days more your government would have to consign me to the grave." In accompanying him over to the office I asked on what conditions was I released. He answered to "give neither aid nor comfort to the enemy." "I will give no such parole, sir, nor has your government any right to ask it. My office is to comfort all who seek comfort of me. As for aid I have none to give excepting I may sometimes have a little more money than I need and this I will give in charity to whom I please, so I will give no such parole." "Well, come over to the office anyhow."

At the commissary's office I had to wait nearly an hour before the Lieutenant in charge of the office came in. After a few words of conversation he remarked, "You are sick, sir." "Yes, Lieutenant. Your government has not only robbed me of my liberty but it has almost robbed me of my life." He then asked me the cause of my arrest, etc. He condemned my treatment in severe language and told me that General Sheridan had ordered my release but I would have to sign a certain paper.

He then opened a long document and commenced reading thus, "I do hereby give my *solemn parole of honor* that henceforth I will deport myself as a good and loyal citizen of the United States." I could keep silent no longer and interrupted, "Lieutenant, that is enough. I will do no such thing. I am no citizen of the United States. I belong to the South and am a chaplain in the Confederate army. I will give no such parole for I will not stop in the United States unless compelled by force. My home is in the South and there I demand to be sent." He then wrote another parole, shorter in matter but not less objectionable. This I also refused to sign. He then looked at the order for my parole and found that I was required to give my parole not to give any military information to the enemy. This I agreed to and the parole was made out to the same effect.

Having signed my paper he asked me if I would like to see the letter of Colonel Harder,* Secretary of Stanton, to General Sheridan. In the letter he speaks of the vile manner in which I was treated in Baltimore and other

---

* Brevet Major General James A. Hardie, U.S.A., his name being misspelled by Father Sheeran. For a while he acted as secretary for the Secretary of War. Perhaps his most notable act while occupying this position was his carrying of the famous message which relieved Hooker of command in favor of Meade just before the battle of Gettysburg.

places and when referring to me always used the term, "Reverend James Sheeran." Sheridan's answer was in a rough, vulgar and boorish style which displayed neither the refinement of a gentleman, the dignity of an educated soldier, nor the feelings of a Christian: "Release *this man* and let him go home if he will give his parole not to give any information to the enemy."

The Lieutenant told me as it was so late that I had better stay in the prison for the night. I told him I had to make a virtue of necessity as I was unable to walk. So I returned to the stable. My companions were really rejoiced to hear of my release, and warmly congratulated me. They treated me with remarkable kindness during this evening, everyone trying to make my last night with them comfortable.

Dec. 5   This morning I feel more composed in mind but more indisposed in body. Having drunk some coffee I prepared for "marching orders," distributed my blankets, mattress and surplus underclothing to the most needy among the prisoners. About 10 a.m. an officer came and informed me in substance that my presence was no longer necessary in prison and that the Provost wished to see me.

Now a very affecting scene took place, for all the prisoners flocked around me to shake hands and bid me goodbye. Seeing them so well disposed I thought I had better say a few words to them. I begged them to draw near and place themselves in order as I wished to speak a few words and was unable to speak loud. I spoke to them of my duties as a Catholic priest: I was bound to do all in my power to promote virtue and correct or restrain immorality. I reminded them of the state of affairs existing when I arrived in the prison, the vulgarity, obscenity then so prevalent. I had first exhorted them kindly but afterwards preached with some severity against these vices. "In thus acting I was actuated by no unkind feeling towards you, but even in my seeming severity had your own interest at heart. As I am about to part from you, never again to see some of you but hoping to meet under more agreeable circumstances I have to thank you for your kindness to me. And if I have said or done anything to wound the feelings of any of you I now publicly ask your pardon. Although I may sometimes look back with feelings of indignation on my sufferings here, I shall often think with pleasure on the agreeable associations found in the Old Stable of Fort McHenry. The books I have lent to some gentlemen I now present to you as a souvenir of our common suffering and sympathies. Wishing our Heavenly Father soon to deliver you and permit you to return to your homes and families I now bid you all goodbye."

When I had reached the outer gate of the prison yard I found that my baggage although small was entirely too heavy for my now reduced strength. I endeavored but in vain to procure a carriage, hack or anything of the kind. I resolved to cross the ferry to St. Michael's. But even this way I had a mile to walk and carry my truck. I reached St. Michael's as near exhausted as I had been in my life. I was warmly received by the whole community.

Father Sheeran spent more than a week with the Redemptorists of St. Michael's Church at Wolfe and Lombard Streets, Baltimore. Then he went to the Redemptorist seminary at Cumberland, Maryland, where he had been ordained in 1858. He remained there until December 19.

Dec. 19   Having been supplied with a good cloth undercoat, a large and comfortable shawl and a good supply of "greenbacks" by the Reverend Father Miller and having bidden them all an affectionate goodbye I left Cumberland at 2 p.m. and reached Martinsburg before dark. Here I intended to stop for the night and start for Winchester by the Pike the following day.

On getting out of the cars, contrary to my expectations, I found myself under guard and had to march to the Provost's office to report. This walk, though short, was one of the most fatiguing of my life. I had a good supply of clothing, etc. rolled up in my oil cloth, indeed almost enough for a pack-mule; besides I had a carpet bag and haversack, all of which I had, as the Southern boys say, "to tote" myself. I had not gone far when I broke down and the guard had to call many times "hurry up." I finally met a German whom I knew. I asked him if he would help me to carry my baggage and I would willingly pay him.

We soon reached the Provost's office where I was kindly treated by my old friend who had before paroled me. He told me I must go to Winchester by way of Harpers Ferry as travelling by way of the Pike is now unsafe for Moseby is about. But he added, "You may stay in Martinsburg as long as you please."

Dec. 20   I said Mass this morning at 7 and prepared to leave but the cars were behind time and did not arrive before night. Harpers Ferry being now a military post and having a large garrison of soldiers I did not like to reach there in the night, fearing I might meet with difficulty. Besides, there are no hotels there nor any other places of entertainment save a few low boarding houses. I was acquainted with Father Costello, the pastor of the place, and with Doctor Morrison* besides a few

* The editor was unable to find more details about the hospitable Dr. Morrison.

other families who lived in the suburbs of the town. Hence, could I reach there in daytime I would feel myself at home, but felt much afraid to reach there after night, being nearly blind, having my own baggage to carry and not knowing when I might be knocked down by some of the robbers of the place. Consequently, I deferred my departure till tomorrow and spent the day very agreeably in company with old friends.

Dec. 21   Say Mass this morning again at 7½ and prepare to start but the cars are again behind time. A telegram is received from some of the upper stations that the cars will not be down before 6 p.m. However I resolved to wait for them this time, reach Harpers Ferry when I may.

There was a large crowd of passengers, mostly Yankee officers, sutlers, and soldiers. Their conversations were on battles fought and victories won over the "rebels," on the bravery of the Union troops and cowardice of the Confederates. It was extremely painful to me to listen to these conversations, particularly when I knew that we had so often chased these very fellows through the Valley as hounds would chase a hare.

At length about 10 the distant whistle of the cars is heard and I rejoice much that I am now to be relieved from my very unpleasant company. In a few minutes more we are on our way for the Ferry. The night is extremely cold, the country covered with deep snow, but an occasional star is seen glimmering through the heavy snow clouds which now hang over this once beautiful but now desolate Valley. We reach Harpers Ferry about eleven p.m. On getting out of the cars I met a guard who asked me for my pass. This I showed him and it being found all right I was told to "move on."

I was now at a loss what to do. It was quite a walk to Doctor Costello's and I was not well able to carry my luggage. To ask any of the soldiers around to carry it for me would betray that I was a stranger and this I did not wish to do.

Whilst thus reflecting a lady who had been in the cars recognized me and asked where I wished to go. I told her any place where I could get shelter for the night as I intended to start for Winchester in the morning. This same person had seen me in Martinsburg when on my way to prison. She pointed to a house with a light, saying she thought I could get accommodations as they kept a boarding-house. I went there but they were "all full." I had now no alternative but to make my way up the steep hill to Doctor Costello's. I have not counted how many times I got out of breath or broke down during this short journey, but often puffing and halting very frequently I reached the Doctor's house almost exhausted. Unfortunately for me the Doctor was in bed and no doubt wrapped in his first sleep. I knocked for some time at the front door and listened with anxious attention for an answer. Sometimes I would imagine I heard the noise of someone within but soon found that the noise was occasioned by the strong wind now sweeping down the Valley. My fingers getting somewhat sore from hard knocking I tried the effect of kicking with my boot heel. But the doctor's sleep was impervious to knocks and kicks. After about half an hour's useless efforts to arouse him I concluded he must not be at home, so leaving my luggage at his door I went down to Doctor Marmien's* some 200 yards distant and knocked there till answered by a sleepy-headed darkey. I asked him if Doctor Costello was at

* Unfortunately unidentified.

home, and, receiving an affirmative answer, back again
I went and tried once more with my boot heels. But
all useless!

I now knew not what to do. The night was extremely
cold and the west wind blowing a piercing blast. There
was no hotel in the place and Doctor Marmien's darkey
would answer me no more for I knocked again at the
door. To walk the streets all night I could not, for no
doubt I would be taken up as a spy. Was I not now in
a pretty pickle? I sat down for a while on the porch
but the piercing wind told me I could not stay here.
I next tried all the doors of the church and sacristy but
they were all secure.

I next went to the *private* house saying to myself "any
port in a storm." But this being built on a high cliff
the wind was blowing through the apertures sharp and
cold enough to take the hide off a fellow, so I cannot
lodge there for the night. I then tried the doors and
windows of the school house but they were proof against
all my efforts. Back again to the porch and tried to
shelter myself by standing up against the door but I
soon began to get cold and tired. Oh, how ardently did
I wish for the morning! But how to spend five long
cold hours was now the query. I was often out at night
before and cold ones too, but never on anything like
this. Besides, on our marches we always had the means
and took the liberty of making a fire. But here there
was nothing of which I could make a fire but the
doctor's out-house (the fences are all rock), and even
did I attempt to make a fire I would arouse the whole
garrison.

Not only the cold wind and the deep snow on the
ground but the whole scenery around was calculated to

give one the "freezes." The doctor's house is on a high
cliff. Beneath it on the south is the Shenandoah now
running high and making a cold grumbling noise.
Beyond the Shenandoah is the Blue Ridge with their
snow-covered summit piercing the low, wintry clouds.
On the north there runs the Potomac now overflowing
its banks and carrying in its rapid course large masses
of broken ice, making anything but a comfortable noise.
Beyond the Potomac are the Maryland Heights with
their cold wintry garments of snow. To the west are
the Bolivar Heights presenting the same bleak and
dismal aspect.

Sleep is now overpowering me and I am compelled
to seek some place of rest. I surveyed the fence corners
till I found a sheltered spot and there resolved to make
my bed. I soon leveled the snow, spread my oil cloth
and blanket, made a pillow of my carpet-bag and covered myself with my shawl; of course I took off no
boots. For a time I felt pretty comfortable as I had on
good warm clothing. But by degrees my feet began to
get cold, next my legs and soon I felt a cold chill pervade
my whole body. Well, thought I, I often heard of people
freezing to death, but I fear I am now about to try the
experiment. Better however, thought I, than to die at
Fort McHenry. Now what can I do to save my life?
Evidently if I remain as I am I must freeze. I soon
remembered having two pairs of drawers in my carpet-
bag and also that Brother Peter had given me a small
bottle, containing about half a gill of the best brandy.
All right, think I, I am not dead yet. I took out the
drawers and rolled one around each foot and leg; and
the brandy, I put it guess where? Anyhow it put my
blood in circulation. I now lay down again, wrapped
myself well up in my shawl, and soon found myself in

the land of dreams waking up only a few times during the remainder of the night to put the clothes in at my back.

When daylight came I thought of remaining in bed that the doctor might see his guest's chamber, but I feared lest I might scare him too much. As I awoke this morning I could hear the crashing of ice in the Potomac as it wended its way to the ocean and the cold, grumbling noise of the Shenandoah as it tumbled over its rocky bed and united its waters with the former river. Were my bed a comfortable one the cold-looking landscape might induce me to enjoy it a little longer, but the truth is I was tired of it. Hence without much reflection I jumped up but was somewhat surprised to find that my legs were not in working order. It was sometime before I got them in motion. I went to the kitchen door and succeeded in waking up the servant. I soon had access to the doctor's room and surprised him in bed. When he saw where I had spent the night I think he felt worse than I did. We soon used means to warm me up and put the blood in circulation. I told him of my intention to start that day for Winchester but this he would not listen to. He told me that for the last two years he was anxious to have a visit from me and now I must spend the Christmas with him. No excuse would be taken. He accompanied me to the commander of the post who told me I might remain as long as I pleased. The doctor did everything he could to make me comfortable but in the afternoon I found that last night's experience was telling on me. I became sick and was compelled to make an early bed-time.

Sunday, Christmas Day   Say my first Mass at 8. Hear some confessions. Say my second Mass at 9½ and my third at 10. Then return to my room. There were no Vespers. The doctor had made ample preparation for Christmas so we spent an agreeable afternoon.

Dec. 26   Say my Mass this morning at 8 and prepare to leave in the afternoon for Winchester. Anticipating some trouble with Sheridan again, for I put little confidence in his official declaration, I asked the doctor to accompany me as it was but a few hours ride by railroad. This he declined to do. About 2 p.m. I repaired to the depot and soon after started for Winchester. I met in the cars one of my fellow-prisoners from Fort McHenry on his way home to his family. He gave me a most consoling account of how the boys behaved themselves in prison after my departure. When any of them would forget themselves some others would only have to remind them of the promises made to Father Sheeran when all would be right again.

We had as fellow passengers on this trip principally Yankee soldiers on their way to their commands. We reached Winchester about 6 p.m. the night being extremely dark.

Dec. 28   This morning as I was able to be around and as I could not walk the streets without a pass I repaired to the Provost Marshal and procured one. My health being now feeble and having a journey of a hundred miles before me I deemed it prudent to rest a few days, so I had my pass extended. I next applied for a pass through the lines in order to have everything ready when my health would permit me to start, but the Provost Marshal referred my application to General Sheridan who now has his headquarters in Winchester.

It would be difficult to describe the feelings of the people of this place on my return from prison. Had I been born and raised among them, and become their best benefactor they could not have given me a more cheerful welcome. There is hardly a family that did not visit me or send me an invitation to call upon them.

Dec. 30   This forenoon General Sheridan sends for me to his headquarters. I now endeavored to brace up my nerves for I was about to "beard the lion in his den." In fact I expected trouble with him although I had a copy of his order for my release. After some formalities I was introduced to a man about five feet six inches high with short legs and long arms, a low forehead and narrow face from about the nose down. In a dry and rather dogged manner he invited me to sit down and then took a seat himself. The following, as near as I can recollect, is the conversation which took place.

General Sheridan, "I understand you want a pass through my lines." "Yes, general, I wish to return home." "Well, you can't pass through my lines." "Why so, general? You ordered my return home on condition I would give my parole to communicate no military information to the enemy. I have given the parole and I demand that you comply with your part of the contract for I consider it a contract which you, in honor and justice, are bound to fulfill." "I never intended that you should pass through my lines." "Well, general, I would like to know what you *did* mean? I have seen your official order and cannot be mistaken. You say, 'Release this man and let him go home if he will give his parole.' Now I would like to know how I am to go home if I cannot pass your lines?" General, "I don't want to argue the point. You will not go South." "There is no point to argue, general, the fact is too plain to require argument. If you meant what you said, you meant I should go home but if you did not mean it the fault is not mine.

I, however, shall hold you to the meaning of your words and shall go home. I am determined to go home, cost what it may. And I think you have given me enough of trouble already not to put me to any more."

There now ensues a short pause which I interrupted by the following question, "Now, general, I have one question to ask you and I hope it will receive an answer. What criminal or ungentlemanly act have I done since I came into your lines that I should be treated in the rough, barbarous, not to say irreligious manner that you have treated me?" He replied, "I don't like the way you came into my lines." "That I cannot help, general. I came in an open, honorable manner with a pass from General Wright which was verbally approved by your adjutant." "I asked my adjutant," says General Sheridan, "and he says he knows nothing about it." "Well, general, if he forgot it I cannot help it. But I give you the word of a gentleman and a Catholic priest that he did approve it." (Here I recalled to Sheridan the very place where I met him and staff.) He still affected to doubt my word. It now became my turn to get a little warm.

I told him very bluntly that as a gentleman I consider my word as good as his or his adjutant's, but in addition I gave him the word of a Catholic priest of good standing in the Church and I thought he had no right to question it. "Besides, I sent you General Wright's pass." "I know you did for I saw it." "Then, sir, why do you insinuate that I came into your lines in a dishonorable manner? General Wright might have arrested me when I applied to him for a pass. This he did not do, however, but on the contrary treated me very kindly and gave me a pass. General, I ask you again and demand an answer, What have I done to deserve this treatment?"

Looking very confused and angry he replied, "Father

Bixio has acted in a manner unworthy of a Catholic priest. He has deceived me and acted meanly." "I tell you I am responsible for my own acts but not for those of any other man." Here he lets off another tirade against Father Bixio, relating what I have already mentioned of the low and very imprudent cunning of this priest.* I now in a tone of indignation remarked that I had long been in the Confederate army and had associated with its most distinguished generals but never was obliged to use any formality with them. Nor do I now feel obliged to use any formality with you. "Hence I tell you candidly, sir, that it is neither fit nor generous on your part to hold me responsible for the conduct of a man of whom I know nothing but that he is a priest." He then somewhat coolly replied, "I know you are not responsible for his acts." "Well, general, since you will not permit me to pass your lines and since I cannot expect any other general of your army to pass on it will you be kind enough to let me know what course I am to pursue?" "You may remain in Winchester as long as you please." "But I do not please to remain here at all. I have no business here as our wounded are all removed." "Well, then, you can go to Baltimore." "No, general, that is not my home. I belong to the South and there I am bound to go. And be assured, General, as long as I remain within your lines I will tell wherever I go that I am a Confederate chaplain and will have to tell, too, how you have treated me. I always thought there was honor among the officers of your regular army. Now, how would it look, in the eyes of all honorable men, were I to desert my command as you suggest by remaining within your lines? Such a dishonorable act shall never stain my character."

* See above, pp. 101–102.

Here the magnanimous Sheridan holds his head a little lower, reflects for a few moments and replies, "I will think about it." "But, General, I would like you to decide upon it. I surely have been long enough under consideration. My means and health will not permit me to remain long here. My case requires medical attention and I wish to repair to the Infirmary at Richmond for that purpose." "Well, I will give you a definite answer tomorrow." So ended my first interview.

I remained in the house the most part of this afternoon, feeling quite unwell. Second interview with Sheridan:

Dec. 31   He received me in a more agreeable tone of voice but without daring to look me in the face. After a moment's pause he said, "I have a few questions to ask you. Do you know Father Bixio?" "I know him, general, but have no particular acquaintance with him." "Does he stop at your house in Harrisonburg?" "No, general, and that for one very good reason, I have no house there or any other place." "Did you see him in Harrisonburg before you came down to Winchester?" "No, general, I have told you in my letter written in prison that I met you and your army this side of Harrisonburg and Father Bixio, I understand, was in the rear of your army." "Well," said he, "Father Bixio has treated me very badly. He engaged as a chaplain in my army, obtained transportation and drew rations as such; he obtained of myself in Harrisonburg a requisition for rations for the sick and wounded alleging that he could distribute them to better advantage than the hospital nurses. Since then I have seen nothing of him but have reason to believe he is corresponding with the enemy." "But, general, why do you implicate me in his actions? If I have any particular fault it is that I am too open and candid in my dealings with my fellowmen. In our limited acquaintance you must perceive that there is no double dealing about me. I am honest and fearless, always doing what I conceive to be my duty without respect to persons. As a chaplain I have always been at my post and have administered the sacraments to thousands of Federal soldiers on the bloody fields of Virginia, Maryland and Pennsylvania."

"I see," said the General, "that I have been mistaken. You may go home when you please. Do you wish to go today? If you do I will send you a pass." "No, General, tomorrow will be Sunday, and I wish to say Mass so I will defer my departure to some day in the beginning of the week." I was about to leave when he told me not to be in a hurry and to keep my seat. He then told me that he was a Catholic himself, that he was sorry to have any difficulty with a Catholic priest, but that no person could blame him for taking care of his own affairs. This then was all the satisfaction made for the injury done me.

1865

Sunday, Jan. 1	This morning hear some confessions, say Mass at 9 and deliver a short instruction to a small congregation. I had many visits today from persons wishing to send verbal messages to their friends within the Confederate army. The weather is extremely cold and I almost dread a journey of a hundred miles on horseback feeling as I do by no means well. But I dreaded still more being within the Yankee lines.
Jan. 2	Have my horse shod this morning and spend the day in making preparations for my journey. During my absence in prison some Irishman belonging to the 18th Pennsylvania cavalry took good care of my horse and consequently he is now in good marching order. But Sheridan had desolated the Valley from Winchester to Harrisonburg so my horse had not only to carry me, my pack of clothing, etc. indeed enough for a pack-mule, but also a sack of oats for himself.
Jan. 3	This morning about 9 having taken a good breakfast, fed my horse well, I mounted (indeed with difficulty as my legs are too short and at that time too stiff) and then bid goodbye to my friends of Winchester never perhaps to see them again.

When leaving town I think I must have presented no very pleasing but somewhat attracting appearance.

I had received some things for Father Smulders, and as I had no permit for them, I had to bring them out for myself. Hence I had to use two hats, one inside of the other. I had, too, a heavy pair of boots for him. These I had to put on myself and hang my own on the front of the saddle. I had swung on my shoulder a large haversack of grub for my journey. I had before me a large sack of oats and behind me a large roll of clothing. You may guess then how I looked. I was almost swallowed in my saddle. At a little distance I am sure no more than my head and shoulders were to be seen.

In a little over an hour by good travelling I made the advanced picket about 6 miles from Winchester. He was a young Irishman not more than six months in this country. He told me I had now nothing to fear as they had no scouts out unless I came across Moseby's men. I laughed at the simplicity of the poor fellow to think that I would be afraid of Moseby or his boys. I was wishing to meet them.

It was now 10 o'clock, the morning extremely cold and I knew of no place to stop this side of Woodstock, some 20 miles distant. And the days being now very short I made up my mind my horse must make that in good time and without feed. This was a lonesome journey and contrasted strangely with the one I made nearly two years ago over this same road on my return from the first Maryland campaign. Magnificent mansions, well-cultivated farms, splendid barns abounding in swine and poultry, herds of cattle in every farm, orchards loaded with autumn fruit, the roads crowded with well-clad and cheerful-looking inhabitants riding to town perhaps on a visit to a neighbor. Such were the objects that then struck the eye.

But now how changed the scene! Houses, barns, stables, haystacks, orchards, fences and every other improvement burned to the ground. The mills too on which the people depended for subsistence are all in piles of ruins. Horses, beef cattle, milch cows, sheep and hogs are all either killed or stolen. There is hardly a cock left to warn the plundered and half-starved inhabitants of the approach of day. Nothing to be seen throughout this vast extent of country but the chimney stacks and charred remains of once splendid mansions. The people in the little towns through which I passed seemed afraid to appear out of their houses.

About noon a heavy snow began to fall. It was accompanied by a strong wind which blew it directly in my face. I used my oil cloth with good effect in keeping off the snow. I now began to feel pains in my legs, no doubt caused by the cold. Indeed the pains increased to such an extent I could not on any occasion dismount from my horse. So I rode the whole day without leaving the saddle.

About 5 o'clock I reached Woodstock and put up with an Irish Catholic named Hays. The gentleman came to the door and very kindly asked me to dismount. I told him I could not without help. He first relieved my horse of the oats bag and then of the other baggage and then aided me in dismounting. It was some time before I could get the blood so far in circulation as to be able to walk to the house. This very hospitable family treated me very kindly and did all they could to make me comfortable.

Jan. 4   I commenced my journey this morning at 10, not wishing to start before the day cleared up. Besides I intended traveling only to Mount Jackson this day, a distance of but eighteen miles. I reached my journey's end about 2 p.m.

Jan. 5   This morning I was on the road early and made Harrisonburg, a distance of 28 miles, about 5 p.m. This day was clear but piercing cold. The frosty wind nearly took the hide off my face, but what the frost did not take off the sun did. About 2 p.m. the sun came out very clear and strong, and strange to say, left my whole face in a blister.

In this town they were well aware of the way Father Bixio fooled Sheridan but I had to tell the people I did not approve of such fooling, if for no other reason than that *I* had to pay too dearly for it.

From the 6th to the 9th I remained here and on the morning of the latter started for Staunton, a distance of twenty five miles. I put up at the house of a German named Shearer to whom I am under many obligations for his kindness. I gave my horse up to the care of the post quartermaster and disposed of my surplus baggage, spurs and saddle, for now I deemed my military career virtually ended.

Jan. 10   Start this morning at 6 o'clock for Richmond and reach there about 6 p.m. I repaired to the Asylum where I was warmly welcomed by the good Sisters, took my supper with them. Next morning I went to the Infirmary and remained there under medical care till the fall of Richmond, suffering much from my breast and eyes.

As I am not writing a history of the war, much less of the Confederacy I will not now attempt an account of the facts which came under my observation during these three months at the Confederate capital. But if the future historian will tell the truth and do his duty, he will hand down the present and the last Confederate Congress to the contempt and scorn of all future generations. They helped much to murder a nation which was winning for itself one of the proudest and most honorable names on record. They tied the hands of President Davis than whom there was never a more disinterested patriot. They clogged the wheels of government. They starved and aided in the demoralization of our noble army. They were great men only in one sense: great in their ignorance and powers to do mischief. Of course, there were a few honorable exceptions among them.

As soon as affairs settled down a little after the occupation of Richmond by the Yankees I obtained a pass and having said my Mass on Easter Sunday morning started for Baltimore in company with thirteen Sisters of Charity. As we passed City Point we heard of the assassination of Abraham Lincoln.

In Washington and Baltimore the excitement caused by his death is so great that I deemed it imprudent to stop so I continued my journey to Philadelphia. From there I went to Reading, Pennsylvania, and visited the *grave of my child*.

April 24   I started this morning for New York and reach there just in time to see the excitement in the city because of Abe Lincoln's remains which were now passing on their way to his former home in the West. The Fathers in New York treated me with every kindness but I found the further I went north the worse my heart was getting. So I took passage on board the steamship George Cromwell, and started for New Orleans on Saturday, April 29.

There was nothing worthy of note on the passage. The weather was fine. As soon as we reached the coast of Florida my health began to improve and continued to improve during the remainder of the trip.

We reached New Orleans on Sunday afternoon, May 7th, after an absence of three years and a half during which time I have witnessed the scenes and events which I have endeavored to narrate in these hastily-written notes.

There exists an alternative traditional account of Father Sheeran's return to his Redemptorist brethren at New Orleans. According to this version, he traveled southward in company with Father Smulders, and *walked* a large part of the way. The account contradicts the narrative given above in Father Sheeran's own words, and is probably over-romanticized. However, as often happens in the case of such traditions, there may be a grain of truth in that part of it which relates the arrival of the two priests at the New Orleans Redemptorist house itself:

One evening there came a hesitant knock on the front door. When a Brother opened the portal he found two priests standing on the doorstep. They wore ragged clothes, were unshaven, and looked dead tired. "We are Fathers Sheeran and Smulders," they said simply, "We have come home from the war." They were welcomed affectionately by the Fathers of the house. Far into the night they were made to sit among their brethren and relate their experiences. They were overcome with joy and relief at being once more in a religious house. They remained at New Orleans for several months, recovering their strength and adapting themselves once again to peace-time life. Then Father Sheeran, rather paradoxically, was given a new assignment in the North.

EPILOGUE

Father Sheeran now served for a few more years at the Redemptorist New Orleans parish. We are not surprised to find him praised by the public press for his selfless devotion and disregard of danger in attending the victims of the city's yellow fever plague of 1867. One can picture him — if the comparison be not irreverent — raising his head like an old war horse at the first scent of trouble, and applying himself to the care of the stricken on this new kind of battlefield.

Shortly afterward, he requested and received a release from his vows as a Redemptorist. As the *Freeman's Journal* later surmised: "Father Sheeran, firm and true to the faith, and its plain demands, had habits too set to make the life of Community, that is of the Rule of St. Alphonsus, pleasant to him."* It seems safe to assume that the parting was effected with amiable feelings on both sides.

Then he did what we might scarcely expect such an ardent Southerner to do — he removed to the North. He became a priest of the Newark (New Jersey) diocese, and in October, 1871, was appointed pastor of the Church of the Assumption, Morristown, New Jersey.

The energy and priestly zeal which he had displayed as a military chaplain had not deserted him. Within a year he had built a new church for his people, and, not long afterward, established a parochial school. The promotion of Catholic education had been always one of his chief passions. In this, the last stage of his career, he dedicated himself to the religious and secular instruction of the "precious little ones," as he called the children.

These details may seem pedestrian when compared with his more spectacular experiences of wartime; but they have their own sym-

---

* April 16, 1881. This same number of the *Freeman's Journal,* asserts that Father Sheeran's son entered the Redemptorist novitiate before his father had done so, and died there. Confirmation of this statement is not available to the present editor of Father Sheeran's *Journal.*

bolism. He was doing what Robert E. Lee, at about the same time, was doing: healing the sectional wounds by placing the nation above section. He had served the people of the South in peace and in war; he would now serve the people above the Mason-Dixon line. He had been a Southern partisan; but he knew that partisanship stops at the boundaries of souls.

He died from a stroke of apoplexy on April 3, 1881.

He may have been, at times, unduly stern and uncompromising. He may have lacked some of the gentler virtues. But, in a world which so readily sells responsilibity for ease, and integrity for profit, we may well prefer Father Sheeran's iron to a more sophisticated irony.

INDEX